MANCHESTER UNITED: MY TEAM

MANCHESTER UNITED: MY TEAM

SAMMY McILROY

SOUVENIR PRESS

First published 1980 by Souvenir Press Ltd,
43 Great Russell Street, London WC1B 3PA
and simultaneously in Canada

ISBN 0 285 62451 2

Printed in Great Britain by
Bristol Typesetting Co. Ltd,
Barton Manor, St. Philips, Bristol

Contents

Photographs by courtesy of Daily Mail: Harry Ormesher:
Daily Mirror: County Press, Wigan: Harry Goodwin: Oldham Chronicle: Owen Barnes: J. Wilson Clarke Photo-
service Ltd: Sunday People

1 Home, Sweet Home. . .

The three worst things that have happened to me in my foot-balling life were the car crash which threatened to bring my career to a premature end, the realisation that we were not, after all, going to win the F.A. Cup final of 1979 . . . and being a young professional with Manchester United.

This latter remark, naturally, deserves some explanation, especially since most Soccer-mad youngsters would give their eye-teeth for the chance of being offered a career at Old Trafford. For love them or hate them, Manchester United have a charisma all their own – and I have to say that now, it would almost break my heart if I were to be told: 'Your services are no longer required here.'

But that was far from being the case when I arrived at Old Trafford from Belfast as a 15-year-old with a fair amount of Soccer talent and, perhaps, not quite enough of the ambition which shrugs aside every other consideration. Believe me, given the chance I would have caught the next boat back to Belfast and settled for a career with an Irish League club. Frankly, life in the big city of Manchester was all too much for me.

It wasn't the bright lights that proved to be a fatal attrac-tion; it wasn't Manchester United's fault, either; in a word, I was homesick. Desperately so. And in those early months of my life on the English side of the Irish Channel, I snatched at every opportunity to return to Belfast, and I would have stayed there without a second thought.

The loneliness of the long-distance runner? – That was nothing compared with the misery I often felt when – as it seemed to me then – I was alone in Manchester, a city whose people went about their own business without a thought in their heads for a lad who, more and more, was becoming con-vinced that he didn't (and never would) belong. I can smile about it now, but at the time those were days of real heartache. And I do not exaggerate when I say that.

Belfast is a city, too, but the people who live there – and no disrespect to them – have a different attitude and a different outlook on life to the folk who live in the big cities in England. In fact, it would not be stretching things too far to say that, compared with Manchester or London, Belfast is more like a town. And I certainly wasn't prepared for the tremendous adjustment it was necessary for me to make when, as a 15-year-old, I crossed the Irish Sea to sign for Manchester United in 1969.

I have to admit that, like so many lads who dreamed of making professional football my career, I also dreamed of the day when I would be asked to join Manchester United. The charisma of the club had cast its spell on me, and as if that were not enough in itself, George Best – who also hailed from Belfast – played for the Old Trafford club. Not that I had ever met him at that time . . . but he was my idol.

I used to go to Mersey Street Primary School, only 50 yards away from my home in Belfast, and I was skipper of the school team in 1965. One season we won just about everything for which we played – we carried off the championship of our league, the cup for which the schools competed, and a cup put up by the evening newspaper in Belfast.

One of the players in that schoolboy side was 'Big Henry' – a centre-half whose name was Henry Blackwood – and you can take my word for it that he was a very powerful player indeed. He didn't just stop our opponents from scoring; he used to go upfield and hammer in goals himself, and we used to say, not without a certain amount of pride, that Big Henry scored more goals than the forwards did – simply by kicking the ball through everyone in front of him. Big Henry still lives in Belfast, and whenever I go back there the odds are that I will bump into him – thankfully, not on the football field. For he's still a big lad now, although he never went into professional football.

One or two of the other lads from that schoolboy side did, though. There was a player called Roy Walsh, and another lad, Ronnie Gray, who went into junior-league football. Ronnie, indeed, had a trial with Manchester United . . . and finished up by returning home, while Roy initially was signed on apprentice forms by United, became homesick, and returned to carve out a career with Glentoran in the Irish League. The end of season 1978–79 saw him collecting the Player of the Year award in Northern Ireland.

From Mersey Street Primary I moved on to Ashfield Secondary, and in the school football team there were two other lads who became professionals with English clubs. John Dempsey finished up playing at centre-half for Chelsea for a lengthy spell, and Eddie Martin became a goalkeeper with Notts County.

By the start of season 1968–69 I was making the breakthrough to international level in the Northern Ireland schoolboy team, and I played in four matches that term – against England, Scotland, Wales and the Republic of Ireland. The tournament ended with the Northern Ireland lads claiming runners-up spot, so we must have had a fair amount of talent in the side.

And it was a talent-spotter who decided that I was going to have what it took to become a professional, for although I was still only 14 years of age, Manchester United's scout in Belfast, Bob Bishop, was keeping an eye on my progress. Bob was the man who first noted the ability of George Best, and there came a day when – ridiculous though it was – I became tagged as 'the new George Best'. But that's another story.

I suppose that I've blessed Bob Bishop and cursed him, at times, for there is no doubt that he was to prove one of the biggest influences in my life. If it hadn't been for him, I would probably never have had the chance to join United; equally, but for Bob, I would never have suffered those bleak spells of homesickness in the early days. So one way and another Bob has something to answer for! But overall, obviously, I owe him a great deal.

Bob had a cottage at Helens Bay, a seaside town which lies about 30 minutes' drive from Belfast, and at week-ends he used to invite myself and a few other Soccer-daft youngsters down there. It didn't matter that in our room there were only three bunks, and perhaps nine or 10 lads – no-one minded sleeping on the floor – and Bob's dog, Dandy, usually managed to find space in one of the bunks, so that meant even more overcrowding. What did matter was the football we enjoyed, and we crammed every possible minute of our waking time into kicking a ball around.

Bob provided the kit and the football, and he didn't try to blind us with science about the tactics of the game. He simply let us get on with the job of enjoying our football. We played in a nearby field or on the beach, and we were without a care in the world as we imagined ourselves to be big-name players. Naturally, in my mind I was always George Best.

Whoever said schooldays are the happiest days of your life must have been thinking about the times when you got out of school and engaged in the business of kicking a football around. That's how it seems to me, at any rate, as I look back, for they were wonderful, carefree days. I wasn't academically minded, and I don't know what I would have done for a living if I hadn't made the grade in professional football. So, as I have said, I owe Bob Bishop a great deal.

I suppose I also owe him a few bob, because it was Bob who bought me my first pair of modern football boots – the ones without the toecaps which used to feel as if they were made of cast-iron. And the day came when Bob asked me if I fancied travelling to Manchester to see how I liked United and how they would like me.

I was excited at the prospect – and apprehensive about it. But I told myself that whatever happened, it would be for only a week during the Easter holidays, so there was no real need to work up a sweat. It was a new and strange experience, but it was a week's holiday spent doing what I enjoyed most, and when I was asked to go back to Old Trafford in the summer, I didn't think twice.

Again I returned home, and the next time it was Manchester United who came to see me. Their chief scout, Joe Armstrong, flew over to Belfast, and I signed the forms that made me an apprentice professional. I had just turned 15.

If it was the biggest moment in my life, it was also a proud moment for my father – his name is Sammy, too – for he had always given me every ounce of encouragement as I pursued my footballing ambitions. And he knew a fair bit about the game himself, for in his playing days he had collected amateur-international caps with Northern Ireland and played at inside-forward, also on an amateur basis, for Linfield, the top club in the Irish League.

When I was still playing primary-school football, my Dad used to offer me 5p for every goal I scored, and as we often won by 10-goal margins, you'll appreciate that I could hardly help but get my name on the scoresheet. In one game I hit eight goals, and my Dad didn't disbelieve me when I asked him, 'How about that, then?' – because he was there to see what had happened with his own eyes.

There had been hints that Everton fancied signing me, and I knew for certain that United's great rivals, Manchester City, were interested in me, for their scout in Northern Ireland (Gibby McKenzie, a former player and manager in Irish League football) had been in touch with my family about taking me to Maine Road. But when the chips were down, there could be only one possible winner, and that was Manchester United. So when they came in for me, I signed without a second thought, and looked forward to getting to know stars such as George Best, Denis Law, Bobby Charlton and Paddy Crerand.

However, I suppose that as an only son I had come to depend on the closely-knit family life more than someone who had brothers and sisters and, perhaps, had had to stand more on their own feet early on in life, and while everyone at Old Trafford made me feel very welcome – and I received a special handshake from George Best the day I arrived – I quickly began to wonder just what I had let myself in for, and whether I could stick it out.

Sometimes I trained in the morning and did jobs around the ground in the afternoon; sometimes I was cleaning boots and laying out kit, cleaning out the dressing-rooms and doing other chores before I got down to training. I didn't mind that part of it at all – what didn't appeal to me was all the time which hung on my hands once the day's work had come to an end.

I was installed in digs, and I found that I simply wasn't able to settle, and though I moved from one set of digs to another, things didn't seem to improve. There was nothing wrong with the digs or the people who were providing me with the accommodation . . . the transition from Belfast to Manchester, for a lad of my tender years, was really too much for me to take in and accept.

I felt lonely, and I wasn't cut out to seek the bright lights of the city. And even when I moved into my third set of digs and found myself being given every consideration, in a bid to make me feel at home, I still hankered for Belfast and what I felt was really 'home'.

I don't suppose for a moment that I was the first – or the last – youngster to feel homesick, for many other lads have left their families and gone into digs, either when they joined football clubs 100 miles or more from their own fireside or when they've taken jobs away from the place where they were brought up. I'm certain, however, that no-one pined more for the faces and the fireside he knew, however humble that might have been – and we weren't a wealthy family in Belfast, by any stretch of the imagination.

Even when I finished up in my fourth set of digs I hankered for my home town, and during those months at Manchester United John Aston, who was then coaching there, must have become sick of the sight of me, for every third week or so I would be asking him if it was all right if I went back to Belfast for a few days. So far as I was concerned, THAT was home . . . and I could never wait to get on the plane and see my folks again.

More than once, I was tempted never to return to Manchester. Indeed, I can remember going to watch an Irish League game with my Dad and testing him out. 'You know, the standard of football isn't so bad over here,' I suggested – and if he'd taken me up on it, I would have settled there and then for quitting United and signing for an Irish League club as a part-timer.

But my father, who was well aware of what I meant, would have none of it. 'You'd be wasting your time coming back . . . stay where you are and stick it out,' was his advice – although I suspect that my mother would have been as pleased as punch to learn that I was returning to Belfast for good.

So, with my Dad simply refusing to listen to my suggestions, I would pack my bag and, with a heavy heart, take my departure for Manchester again . . . back to a city where I felt like a stranger. To my way of thinking, I was a misfit. I didn't really know anyone, I was missing my home and my parents, and the people themselves seemed so different to the ones I knew back home. When I wasn't asking John Aston if I could go over to Belfast for a flying visit, I was spending my evenings phoning the folks at home, watching television or kicking a ball around with some lads in the street where I was in digs.

Yet somewhere, deep down, there must be a stubborn streak in me, for never once did I let on to people at Old Trafford how miserable I was feeling when I was away from the club. When John Aston asked me if I was missing home, I would answer honestly and say 'Yes', but I tried never to let him see just how badly – although he must have suspected, from the number of times I hopped a plane to return to Belfast. Maybe he even wondered if the day would come when there would be a phone call from me to say I was never returning. But I always did arrive back.

I have to say, also, that today United – who always did have a name for being good to young players – go out of their way to make sure that lads signed by them are not left on their own when they first arrive at Old Trafford. Often enough, someone from the club – chief scout Joe Brown, Norman Davies or Norman Scholes – will go round to the digs and take the youngsters to the cinema or spend some time having a chat with them.

Oddly enough, when I first arrived at Old Trafford it was in company with another lad from Belfast. His name was Drew Harris and, like me, he signed apprentice forms. He seemed to settle much better than I did – I suppose we're all made differently – and even though he was eventually given a free transfer and drifted out of professional football, he still lives close to the ground, at Stretford. Now he plays football in a Sunday league, and sometimes we meet each other. In fact, Drew still goes to watch United play, so he counts himself as one of the thousands of fans.

A young Scot who joined United was Frank McGivern. He signed apprentice forms at the same time as myself, and when he was given a free transfer from Old Trafford, he moved on to Middlesbrough. Like Drew Harris, Frank dropped out of League football, though we keep in touch – indeed, when I married, he was best man.

Despite my initial homesickness, two things were motivating factors when it came to my staying at Old Trafford. There was my father's insistence on my not chucking up the sponge and settling for a part-time role in football back in Belfast, and there was the fact that while I had attended a couple of schools, at the age of 15 I realised without a doubt that I had had virtually no schooling. That wasn't the fault of the teachers, I hasten to add; it was simply that when I left school I wasn't equipped for a job which would have brought me a good wage. I was unskilled, and if I had left full-time football, I would have had to take on some kind of manual job.

My Dad put matters succinctly when he told me : 'You're going to make it in football – and where you are (meaning Manchester United) is the place to make it.' His words rang in my ears, and the knowledge that if I didn't make it in football I would be going into a factory job was the clincher. So I soldiered on.

Eventually, I found two solutions to the problem of loneliness and being homesick – I got married, and I organised things so that my parents were able to move from Belfast and live in Manchester – a little more than a stone's throw from Old Trafford, as a matter of fact. Looking back, I would have got my folks over much earlier, especially with the troubles that were brewing in Northern Ireland, but it all worked out satisfactorily enough. I managed to find them a little house and was fortunate enough to be able to borrow the cash to finance the move.

And marriage? – That was the best thing that happened to me, although I'm not making this an argument for every teenage footballer to start looking for a wife as soon as he joins a club. I was only 16 years old when I first met Cynthia, the girl who was to become my wife, and it was a chance affair, because as I have mentioned earlier, I'm not one for the bright lights. You couldn't say I was living it up when I decided to go to a club not far from Old Trafford one night – some of the lads were fairly regular visitors, and I was persuaded to join them.

Frank McGivern was keeping me company that evening, and the event was a fancy-dress dance. The United players and myself went as ourselves, dressed casually . . . Cynthia was there and dressed up as an Indian. It turned out that the D.J. was someone I knew slightly, and when I mentioned the girl in the Indian get-up he told me he knew her – so I asked him to drop the hint that I'd like to talk to her.

When we did get chatting, the end of the evening was in sight, and we made a date to meet again the next night. We went out together for several months, then came the parting of the ways, and I must say I thought that was the end of that. But a couple of months later I went back to the club 'on spec' – and Cynthia was there.

She was dancing with a friend . . . and I was sat there like a dummy, because I'd broken an arm in a training mishap. But though I couldn't dance, I could talk, and we got chatting. The romance was on again, and we finished up getting married. In fact, the last digs in which I lived were her home, for I was invited to stay with the family once it was established that we were courting seriously. We were married before long – I was 18, Cynthia was 19 – and by then homesickness had become a thing of the past.

I now look upon myself as a Mancunian by adoption, and for me, Manchester does mean home. We live in a house about 10 minutes' drive from Old Trafford – Bobby Charlton lived there before us – and it couldn't be more convenient. I can afford to smile now when I think how easily I might have given up and gone back to Belfast during those early months of my life in Manchester, and my career at Manchester United has brought me so many memories – a few sad moments, but a lot of happy ones.

2 'The New George Best'

I take some pride in being able to claim that I am the last of the famous Busby Babes, for I am now the only player who, as a schoolboy, joined the club when Sir Matt Busby was still the manager and stayed the course through the various upheavals Manchester United have known during the past decade or so – and there have been quite a few.

I took no pleasure, in the early days of my breakthrough to first-team football, in being tagged 'the new George Best'. It never was my idea to try to emulate the player who had been my idol, for our styles of play were different, for a start. For another thing, so far as I was concerned, there could be only one George Best – he was the original, and anyone trying to become a copy was bound to end up looking like a very pale imitation.

I don't know how I came to be called 'the new George Best'; I do know that I felt it was unfair even to suggest that I was in the same bracket as George, because from the start, it could only put me under extra pressure. And trying to break through to United's first team was difficult enough, without such comparisons being made. Even if I looked like him in appearance or, occasionally, in the way I played, I could never have kept it up.

For a start, George was a great tackler and a great header of the ball, and no way were those among my strong points. Nobody needed to tell me that as an all-round footballer, he was one in a million. It got me down when I read that I was being tipped to become a success in the same, sensational manner as George had done, and when I did start playing in the first team, the fact that I scored in my first four games weighed heavily on me, too, for I knew better than anyone that this was beginner's luck, as it were, even if I had played quite well.

I had met George once, before I arrived at Manchester United – a brief introduction by Bob Bishop and a handshake before a Northern Ireland international match against Scotland at Windsor Park – but the handshake I received from George on the day I made my first-team debut for Manchester United meant even more. I was just 17 and, eight years previously, George had also made his first-team bow at the same age. Though that, really, was where the similarity ended.

I won't deny that I was overawed – perhaps even a bit frightened – when I arrived at Old Trafford at first as an apprentice professional and found myself surrounded by so many star names. Denis Law and Paddy Crerand had a few words for me and helped to make me feel a bit more at home, but I was too nervous to become starry-eyed, for I knew that I was still very much on trial.

In those days, it was really something to take part in a five-a-side game and realise that household names such as Crerand, Law, Best and Charlton were actually passing the ball to you. One thing I learned quickly, as well: there was a difference whenever I went home to Belfast . . . because a lot of people I had hardly known made a point of coming up to me and talking football. Just because I had signed for Manchester United.

I suppose it all depends upon your make-up as to how you react. Under such circumstances, it's easy enough to regard yourself as someone a bit special, and to become bigheaded. In my case, though, while I enjoyed talking to people about Manchester United, I had to live with the knowledge that they could stay home while I had to go back to the big city and live with that loneliness I mentioned earlier, so there was no danger of my being carried away by the aura of glamour. Already I had experienced the heartache side of football.

It took me 18 months to settle, and in that time I had started courting and finished up getting married. But I still had to make my way in football, and although I had become a regular in the reserve team, the competition was fierce. At the time I arrived at Old Trafford, in 1969, these were the stars who were regarded as first-team regulars, or members of the senior pool of players :

Alex Stepney, Shay Brennan, Tony Dunne, Paddy Crerand, Bill Foulkes, Nobby Stiles, Willie Morgan, Denis Law, Bobby Charlton, George Best, Johnny Aston, Carlo Sartori, Francis Burns, David Sadler, Don Givens, Jimmy Ryan, Alan Gowling, Steve James, John Fitzpatrick, Jimmy Rimmer, Paul Edwards, Ian Ure and Brian Kidd . . . you could pick the bones out of that lot, and have two top-class teams.

A formidable array of talent – and, for a 17-year-old, it represented a tough job when it came to realising his ambitions of staking a claim for a first-team place. When the day did arrive, it came in a manner I had never anticipated . . . and it began with me being in the mood to storm out of Old Trafford and catch the plane back to Belfast. Not because I was homesick this time, but because I thought I was being given the cold-shoulder treatment.

The biggest match of the season in Manchester is the local derby game, when United tangle with City, and on this particular occasion the game was scheduled for Maine Road, on a Saturday afternoon. The previous night, at Old Trafford, the mini-derby was due to be played, between the reserve sides of the respective clubs, and I was looking forward to the action in that match.

I had graduated to the reserves at 16, via the A and B teams, and felt I had established myself as a regular in the Central League side by the time I was 17. I had travelled to Switzerland and played for the youth team in a tournament there, and things seemed promising all round, now that I was settled at last in the big city.

By then, Matt Busby had relinquished the job of team manager, Wilf McGuinness had been and gone, and Frank O'Farrell was in the chair. Bill Foulkes was helping out on the backroom side, and on the afternoon of the derby game between the reserve teams he collared me and told me I wouldn't be playing that night. He added that the following morning I had to report to Old Trafford.

Inwardly, I was seething. I knew I hadn't done anything

wrong, and had been confidently expecting to play in the mini-derby game. Now I had been told, in a roundabout way, that I had been dropped from the reserves. For two pins I could have got up and walked out of Old Trafford and caught the plane to Belfast . . . but I didn't. Instead, I said nothing, though I felt miserable.

The way I read the situation, I was being ditched from the reserves and used as some kind of messenger on the Saturday morning – maybe to pick up some kit or do some other chore – and Bill didn't enlighten me, though when I bumped into Frank O'Farrell he just told me to make sure that when I reported at Old Trafford next morning I was wearing a collar and tie.

I still didn't realise the significance of all this, and I was feeling disgruntled when I left the ground, though I had decided there was nothing else for it but to do what Bill Foulkes and the boss had said. My mood hadn't changed when I returned to Old Trafford on the Friday evening and sat through the 90 minutes of the mini-derby. I still reckoned that whatever job they had waiting for me on the Saturday, I could and should have played for the reserves that night.

The next morning my mood hadn't improved much as I went down to the ground, and then it all began to make sense as I walked into the kitchen for a cup of tea, for the people there were smiling and wishing me all the best . . . and it dawned on me that they were talking about me playing in the BIG one that afternoon.

The man whose place I would be taking was Denis Law – he had had to drop out because of an injury – which meant that I was playing up front alongside Bobby Charlton and George Best. The team that derby day read : Stepney, O'Neil, Dunne, Gowling, James, Sadler, Morgan, Kidd, Charlton, McIlroy, Best. And the substitute was John Aston . . . who was aggrieved because he felt that he should have been playing from the start of the match.

John had a point, too, because he was recognised as the regular 12th man, and I could appreciate his feelings, for only hours earlier I'd been unhappy about losing my place (as I had thought) in the reserve side. But John held no grudge against me and we both knew that in the final analysis the manager is the guy who picks the team. Frank O'Farrell had made his decision, for better or for worse, and I was making my debut.

I suppose I'll never know what made Frank O'Farrell decide to pitch me in at the deep end – you just don't ask the manager that kind of question – but it was suggested that a hat-trick I had scored in a five-a-side competition in London earlier in the week had earned me the vote, once it was known that Denis Law was out of the derby game. And what kept him out? – a bruised toe . . .

If United had taken a gamble, so had Manchester City, for one of their key players, England-international Colin Bell, had been rushed into hospital only 72 hours before the big match. He had injured a knee playing against Sheffield United, and it had turned septic, so City whipped him in for hospital treatment. And he played. The City team that day contained a lot of star names, too : Corrigan, Book, Donachie, Doyle, Booth, Oakes, Summerbee, Bell, Davies, Lee, Mellor. And City's substitute was Neil Young.

While I was sitting in the Maine Road dressing-room awaiting my first-team debut, the fans were rolling up in force – there were 63,000 people inside the ground when the referee signalled the start of the match. It turned out to be an explosive derby game, too, especially in the first half, when three players had their names taken by the referee. Two of them – Franny Lee and Tony Book – wore City's colours, and Tommy O'Neil was the United player to be cautioned.

But it was my name that hit the headlines that evening, for I scored the first goal in a game which produced five more goals and a 3–3 scoreline. It was a sizzling match, right the way through . . . although for the first quarter of an hour I was wondering if every match in the First Division was played at such a tempo. City set about United from the kick-off, and we were run off our feet in those first 15 minutes.

Malcolm Allison was City's team manager then, and he never made any secret of his desire to see United buried by The Blues. And buried we almost were in the early part of the game, as City produced such fluent football that they seemed certain to score – and if they did, it looked like opening the floodgates.

Our defenders were back-pedalling time after time, as City drove forward: Mike Doyle headed one effort over the bar, Alex Stepney saved a cross from Ian Mellor at the foot of a post, and Wyn Davies powered a header from a Summerbee cross just over the top. Then Franny Lee missed a chance to give City the lead when, with only the United 'keeper to beat, he shot straight at Alex Stepney, and minutes later City fans roared for a penalty as a shot from Mellor struck O'Neil.

Lee did get the ball in the net, but the referee – it was Ray Tinkler, I remember – disallowed a goal for an offence, and after we had somehow survived that opening assault, we began to get into the game ourselves. The first booking came when Tony Book fouled Alan Gowling, and the United player went head over heels; a couple of minutes later, and I was sent sprawling by an opponent, then George Best was going down – a foul which brought a ticking-off for Alan Oakes from the referee.

That foul brought United a free-kick two yards outside City's 18-yard box, and when Brian Kidd teed up the ball for Bobby Charlton, he hammered in a drive which cannoned off the wall of City defenders and reached George Best . . . who promptly shot and saw his effort flash wide of a post. Just after half an hour's play, Franny Lee's name went into the book when he fouled George, though the City man made it clear that in his opinion, George had 'dived' when the tackle was made.

The game was rapidly reaching boiling point, since no-one on either side was prepared to give quarter – and nobody was asking for it, either – then there was a crescendo of sound from the United supporters, five or six minutes before half-time, as I put the Reds ahead. We had been outplayed for most of the half, but in a quick attack Bobby Charlton and George Best linked up and, as Book tried to halt George, my team-mate rolled the ball back in my path. I hadn't time to stand and stare – and maybe miss the chance. I just drilled a shot for goal, and the ball sped past Joe Corrigan.

With half-time looming, Tony Dunne and Mike Summer-bee tangled, and the United defender was carried to the touchline with an ankle injury, so John Aston did get his chance to play in the derby game from the restart. And within a minute of the second half getting under way, United were two goals ahead, as Bobby Charlton and George Best once more joined forces down the left side of the field.

As George crossed the ball low into the middle, there was a fleeting chance for me to make some kind of history by claiming my second goal, but I knew that Brian Kidd was placed even better to do some damage, and I stepped over the ball, leaving my United team-mate with the opening. Joe Corrigan seemed to trip and fall as Brian set himself up for the shot, and again the United faithful hailed a goal, while the City fans were silenced.

But City were far from finished, and when Mike Summer-bee made a run he got across a centre which Mike Doyle reached . . . only to head inches over the top of the United bar. Five minutes into the second half, and City had a goal disallowed for the second time in the game, but in the 58th minute Franny Lee pulled one back for them from the penalty spot, after he had been brought down by Tommy O'Neil. The spot-kick was so fierce that Alex Stepney had no chance.

Five minutes or so later, and the scoreline read 2–2, as Colin Bell justified City's gamble on his fitness by knocking in an equaliser when he took the ball round United's 'keeper and tapped it home, and the excitement continued as John Aston made it 3–2 to United, then Mike Summerbee hit an equaliser again for City, with just four minutes of that 85th derby game remaining.

I've played in many derby games since, but that one was the most memorable. I can still see myself sitting in the dressing-room before the kick-off, still hear Brian Kidd's words of advice – he must have been all of 21 – as he told me to go out and simply play my own game. Bobby Charlton echoed this advice to me, as well. And in the team coach on the way to Maine Road, I noticed that the fans making their way to the ground were looking up and identifying the various

United players – until they spotted me. Then, no doubt, they were asking each other : 'Who's he?'

A couple of other things about that match stand out in my mind. There was a confrontation in the tunnel at half-time between Frank O'Farrell and Mike Summerbee, with United's manager complaining about the injury which had put Tony Dunne out of the game for the second half, and on a happier note at the end George Best came over to me and said that he hadn't forgotten the promise he had made to me before we went out. He'd be in with the bottle of bubbly on the Monday. For George had promised to treat me to a bottle of champagne if I scored a goal. And he was true to his word.

That point kept Manchester United at the top of the First Division table, and with Denis Law still out of action 48 hours later I stayed in the side for a League Cup replay at Stoke, and made my home debut the following Saturday against Spurs. And scored another goal.

Denis Law was back by then, but Brian Kidd was out through injury, so I kept my place, and when I hit the ball home after the game had been going for 40 minutes 54,000 fans yelled their delight. Tottenham's last line of defence was another footballer from Northern Ireland, Pat Jennings, and though I didn't know it then, it wouldn't be long before he and I were playing as team-mates at international level. That day, however, Pat and his team-mates finished on the wrong end of a 3–1 scoreline, as Denis Law celebrated his return with a brace of goals.

Denis had some nice things to say about me after the game, but what struck me most was the way that one or two matches can build a player up so that people come to expect a great deal from him. My game against Spurs was only the third for United's first team – yet after just one week it was being suggested that I was ready for international honours. 'Sammy McIlroy should soon be called on to stand side by side with George Best to wear the green of Ireland,' was how one writer put it.

And Denis Law reminded people : 'It's little more than a week since Sammy McIlroy arrived on the scene. Yet now he is known throughout the country.'

Heartwarming stuff . . . but you know what they say about a little learning being a dangerous thing! When fame comes suddenly, there is always the temptation for a youngster to think not only that he's got it made, but that he knows it all. At the time that United scored their 3–1 win over Spurs they were leading the First Division by three points . . . yet relegation wasn't so far away, as things turned out. For a player, sudden recognition can be exciting, and the name of the game may appear to be glamour; but the glitter can fade all too quickly, if you let yourself get carried away by praise.

Fortunately, I had sufficient sense to realise that it's your next game that counts, and I was willing to keep on learning – even though I kept my place in the side for a game at Southampton, and scored one of the goals in United's 5–2 victory. There was a reminder, also, that I was still a kid playing a man's game in the fact that I was a member of United's youth side, and a few days after the trip to The Dell I was playing against Everton in the F.A. Youth Cup.

After drawing 1–1 at Old Trafford, we went to Goodison Park for the replay. Not only did we lose, 2–1, but that match taught me another lesson, for it was one in which I received a booking. I've tried to ensure that I've stayed out of trouble for the most part ever since.

3 A Shouting Match

I once played truant from school to watch Manchester United play. They were over in Dublin for a friendly match against Bohemians, the League of Ireland club, and I travelled down from Belfast to see the stars who, even after 90 minutes, were still just names to me. Later, I got to know them well, although it took a considerable time before I appreciated Bobby Charlton.

Bobby always seemed a man of few words, in my early days at Old Trafford, and for quite a while I thought that he was a bit stand-offish. As I came to know him better, I realised that here was a fellow who let his football do the talking for him, and that, if anything, off the field he was rather shy until he got to know you. In some ways, I think, Bobby and I were two of a kind – we tended to be reserved, rather than outgoing.

Other players who were in United's team when I arrived at Old Trafford were different. Alex Stepney always had a strong sense of fun, and he was one of the dressing-room jokers. I remember a tour abroad, not long before he left Old Trafford to start a new career in American Soccer, when he pulled a fast one on Ashley Grimes.

We were in Bermuda at the time, and Alex fixed up with a local policeman to come into the bar where we were having a drink and ask for Ashley. I was in on the joke, and when the copper – wearing plain clothes – walked in that was the cue for me to say to him: 'Leave my mate alone . . . we're playing darts.' When the policeman produced his identity card and asked Ashley to accompany him to the station, I chipped in with my set speech, while Alex was almost falling about laughing, and Ashley, becoming more and more agitated, turned on me and said: 'I'll do my own talking.'

Once he realised it had all been a put-up job he gave Alex a real piece of his mind.

They say that it's the secret ambition of every comic to play Hamlet, and when it comes to goalkeepers, there is nothing more they enjoy than playing outfield during practice matches. Alex Stepney was no exception – and he was one of the best marksmen I have seen in five-a-side games. He scored goals with flicks and headers, and was always the first player to be chosen by the skipper who had first call.

Tony Dunne and Shay Brennan, who were full-back partners for a lengthy spell, were opposites. Tony was always quiet, while Shay was ebullient, and enjoyed nothing more than to have a flutter. We used to say that the White City greyhound-racing stadium was his second home. Paddy Crerand was another of the players who was always ready to crack a joke, though he really took his football seriously, and I won't argue with anyone who claims that when Paddy was on song, so were United. His passing was tremendous, and if he gave the ball away four times in a match he'd had a bad game.

Bill Foulkes had switched from playing to a backroom role by the time I was in the reserve side, and apart from that derby-game incident I have mentioned, I remember Bill for another incident when United were playing a pre-season friendly match against Winsford United, in the Cheshire League.

Bill, who was a hard man himself when he played in defence for United, knew how the opposition would react when they came up against us, and he didn't mince his words. 'Play it the same way as they do, and get stuck in,' was his advice.

We were leading by the only goal of the game, and I collected the ball out on the wing. I went on a dribble, and lost the ball, and the next thing Bill was shouting at me from the dug-out. I simply lost my head, and stood there, shouting back at him, while my team-mates watched us in amazement – and Winsford took advantage of this to set up an attack. Before we realised what had happened, they were down at our end of the field and they almost scored a goal.

At the end of the match, Bill gave me a real telling-off

about holding on to the ball and losing it. By then, I'd cooled down and I took his point. And I have to say that while he may have been a hard man himself, he was also fair – and one of the best fellows in the game at getting players in peak physical condition.

I remember Willie Morgan for his skill and quiet humour – and for the football boots he wore, because he had a pair made by a certain manufacturer, and he asked me if I would fancy wearing boots like them. I was due to play for Northern Ireland in the home-international series, and Willie gave me a pair of red boots, saying: 'See what they're like; and if you fancy them, then you can wear 'em.'

I took the boots home, and my wife did the packing for me as I prepared to travel to Belfast. When I arrived, I discovered that they were the only boots she had thrown into my grip, so it was Hobson's choice. I was substitute for that particular match, and I sat on the bench wearing my red boots and thinking of the ribbing I had had to take from the other players.

Then Eric McMordie came off the park and I had to go on, and as soon as the fans saw the colour of my boots they began to give me some stick. Tommy Cavanagh, who became Danny Blanchflower's right-hand man with the international team, was sitting in the stand that day and he told me afterwards that whenever he thinks of me he recalls a pair of skinny legs and those vivid red boots at the end of them. I never wore those boots again – though I cracked on to Cav that I'd earned fifty quid for playing in them.

I remember an occasion when, during the reign of Frank O'Farrell as manager at United, Denis Law was named as substitute – and Denis sat in the dressing-room right through the game. He said: 'If anyone wants me, they know where I am.' Denis liked to be playing – or out of the way. He didn't like watching a match (he was missing from the team coach the day I made my debut in his place), and he wasn't happy being named substitute. So far as he was concerned, he wanted to be playing, even if it meant second-team football. That day he stayed in the dressing-room, his services were not required, as it happened.

George Best? – Well, there's no need to remind anyone of the tremendous talent he brought to Old Trafford, nor to dwell on the off-the-field activities which, from time to time, made him headline news. But whenever I think of George, I am reminded of the time I was chosen to make my international debut for Northern Ireland, and he told me not to worry about the tickets for travelling to Hull for the game.

I'd seen George in town on the Saturday night and arranged to meet him at the railway station for the trip to Hull. I arrived at the station in good time, and I waited until the last possible minute . . . but there was still no sign of George. So I dashed to the booking office and got my own ticket. And, of course, I arrived at Hull without him.

Not surprisingly, the Irish team manager – at that time it was Terry Neill – asked me where George was, and I simply told Terry that I'd made my own way to Hull. It turned out that George had completely forgotten about the arrangement he had made to meet me at the railway station, and he travelled by car to Hull. When I reminded him that he was supposed to have been getting the tickets, he was full of apologies.

In spite of that incident – and I'll admit I wasn't very pleased about having to dash and get my own ticket at the last moment – I always liked George. Off the field, he was so quiet it seemed that butter wouldn't melt in his mouth. But it is no less than the truth when I say that people – and I'm not referring to those inside the club – never left him alone. There always seemed to be someone wanting to talk to him or take a photograph of him or collect his autograph.

Plenty of people have asked me for my autograph over the past 10 years, but I know that it's been nothing like the same as it was for George, who – like it or not – got caught up in the big-time. And when you're single, people expect you to have plenty of free time to attend functions and so on. Which means that apart from not having ready-made excuses for saying 'No, thanks', you also have the ever-present temptation to indulge in a hectic social life.

In my case, I was married young and when children come along you have that feeling of added responsibility. In addition, it was a comparatively simple thing for me to bring my parents over to England. George had brothers and sisters, as well as his parents, and it was probably too much to expect the whole family to settle in the Manchester area. In any event, George was one on his own, an enigma in so many ways. Yet I couldn't help but like him, apart from admiring his footballing skill.

Don Givens was another Irishman whose career began at Old Trafford, and when I arrived he was already playing for the Republic of Ireland international side and knocking on the door of the first team at United. Perhaps I was lucky, in that players such as Denis Law and Bobby Charlton were coming towards the close of their top-class careers when I made the breakthrough; in Don's case, while he got a chance he never really had an extended run in the senior side, since Denis and Brian Kidd were the established front-line men, alongside George Best, and Alan Gowling was another contender for a place in the attack.

Don eventually moved on to Luton, and he gave them fine service before playing for Queen's Park Rangers and Birmingham. And in my time at United I've seen a lot of players come and go, while I have served under five team bosses – Matt Busby, Wilf McGuinness, Frank O'Farrell, Tommy Docherty and Dave Sexton.

I didn't see a great deal of Matt Busby when he was manager, as it turned out. Joe Armstrong travelled to Belfast to sign me, we flew back to Manchester and I was introduced to the man who had done so much to create the image of greatness at Old Trafford. I wondered if he really was as great as people seemed to think, and all I can say now, after 10 years with Manchester United, is that I have never known anyone at the club have a bad word to say about him. Which is sufficient tribute in itself.

He took me on a club tour to Dublin when United played Bohemians, and I played in that friendly match. I was only 16 then, and it was a thrill to pull on the famous red jersey and I felt made up when I scored a goal. Matt Busby just told me to go out and enjoy myself, as he has told countless other players, and it was nice to see what he said about me after I had made my First Division debut. 'I've been talking about this boy for two years . . . he really excites me.'

So far as I know, Matt Busby has played fair with me ever since, and, indeed, I have never known him let anyone down. To put it in its simplest terms, I regard him as a great man.

When he stepped down from the manager's chair, it was in character for him to want to keep the job in the family, and I'm certain he hoped with all his heart that Wilf McGuinness would follow on and stay in charge of team affairs for many years to come. Sadly for both men, it didn't work out like that.

Wilf was keen on giving youth its chance, and I know that he also wanted to buy some players. The major problem for him, I am convinced, was that he was brought in at the top and there were quite a few players who had been contemporaries of his on the park. So it was a difficult situation from the start. Those senior players found it hard to take orders from someone who, not so far back, had been a team-mate, and under circumstances such as those I think that a manager's authority is bound to suffer to some extent.

Personally speaking, I never had cause to complain about Wilf McGuinness, and I have always felt that, given the conditions under which he was operating, he did a pretty good job. It was tough enough to follow in the footsteps of Matt Busby without having to face up to the problems of maintaining his own authority.

I cannot have any grouse about Frank O'Farrell, either – apart from anything else, he gave me my chance of First Division football and that was a big thing for a 17-year-old. We had a spell during his time at Old Trafford when it looked as if we were going to be in with a shout for the League championship, but when results began to go the other way the picture was not so bright.

Confidence began to wane, and Frank was a quiet character, even when everyone was shouting the odds about United winning the title. It wasn't in his nature to change and, if anything, he seemed to me to become more withdrawn as the pressures became greater. The players didn't see him as much, and eventually the day came when we saw him no more. As had happened with Wilf McGuinness, he left Old Trafford.

There was one incident involving me during Frank O'Farrell's period as manager which hit the headlines, and it concerned a club tour of Israel. Instead of flying out with United, I caught another plane – to Belfast. And the word got around that I had defied the club, had a row, and gone off in a huff. It didn't happen quite like that, though.

For me, season 1971-72 had been a long and gruelling slog. I was still only 17, had been breaking my neck to ensure that I kept my place in the first team, and the effort of doing so had taken its toll. I should have joined my team-mates, Denis Law and Martin Buchan, at London airport on the Sunday, and at that moment in time the intention was that I would go on the tour. But I felt so whacked that after going to bed in Manchester on the Saturday night I didn't awake until it was too late to make the connection to London.

Denis and Martin had travelled there after being on international duty with Scotland; I had been with United's youth team to the Continent, then played for the Northern Ireland side in the home internationals. And apart from the fact that I overslept, I was worried because I had learned that my father wasn't well. When I explained matters on the phone to Frank O'Farrell, I asked if I could be excused from going on the trip to Israel and, instead, fly home to Belfast to see my parents and, at the same time, get a real break from football. The manager saw my point of view, and agreed.

United were already in Tel Aviv, and Frank explained in a statement just what had happened, so there was no real mystery about it. United made it clear that no disciplinary action would be taken against me, and that was the end of that. However, the manager was more concerned about another absentee Irishman . . . George Best.

George, who had earlier announced that he was turning his back on football, was in one of his favourite haunts, Spain. He was said to be on vacation at Marbella until June, then be likely to move on to Magaluf, in Majorca. Frank O'Farrell's statement from Tel Aviv said he was 'very upset' about George's failure to join United, for he had expected him to keep to the terms of his contract and play in Israel. It was another incident in the long-running saga of George Best and Manchester United.

As for me, I returned from Belfast feeling refreshed and ready for the new season, and in November, 1972, I took the plunge and got married. Two months later Cynthia and I were involved in a car crash, United had a new manager – Tommy Docherty – and I was wondering if I would ever play top-class football again.

The car crash happened close to home, and it was a serious one. In fact, firemen had to be called to free us from the wreckage although, fortunately, Cynthia was able to go home after treatment at the hospital, and the driver of the other vehicle was not detained in hospital. But I was, and when I was examined under an anaesthetic, it was discovered that I was suffering from broken ribs and a collapsed lung. I also had stitches put in wounds to my head and face, and when I finally began to think about football again, it was with the knowledge that I was unlikely to play again for the rest of that season – and who knew what the future held, come to that?

The immediate bad news was that I would be certain to miss three matches in the World Cup qualifying stages for Northern Ireland and the three home-international games. The good news came when I was assured by the doctors that despite my injuries – four broken ribs and that punctured right lung – there was no threat to my career in the long term. I had caught the full impact of the crash, and I was told later that my fitness probably saved my life.

I was forbidden to train, and allowed only to walk when I made my exit from the hospital, and I found that I had trouble breathing, while any kind of jerky movement hurt. Coughing, for instance. I still harboured some doubts about the shape my Soccer career would take when I finally regained full fitness, and in the meantime I had some worries about Cynthia, who was expecting our first child, because she was admitted to hospital again, this time suffering from high blood pressure. Fortunately, there were no problems there, and Manchester United were good enough to offer to send the two of us on holiday to Switzerland so that I could recuperate at leisure.

By mid-March I was still awaiting the all-clear to resume training – and I had discovered that my lung and ribs were not the only casualties of the crash. For occasionally my back would become itchy . . . and I learned that this was because embedded in it were seven slivers of glass. When I scratched my back one day, a sliver fell out, and in time the other half-dozen did the same.

It's strange when you reflect on little decisions which can turn out to be unexpectedly important. The accident wouldn't have happened, for instance, if I hadn't decided I'd like some chips for tea, and I thought I'd save Cynthia the trouble of making them. So we were on our way to the chip shop when – crash! It meant eight days in hospital for me, and a loss of half a stone in weight.

Five months of gnawing doubt and anxiety finally ended for me when I was given the go-ahead to play for Manchester United in a youth tournament in Switzerland in the May. For some weeks beforehand, I had been able to kick a ball around and do some training, but all the time at the back of my mind had been the knowledge that the doctors were constantly telling me: 'Don't take chances and play in a full-scale match.' So the clearance to play in the youth tournament lifted a load of worry off my mind.

At the same time, I knew that I wasn't out of the wood by quite a long way, because I didn't really know United's new boss, Tommy Docherty – except by reputation. And that showed him to be a wheeler-dealer in the transfer market. The question was: would I be one of the players The Doc decided to clear out from Old Trafford?

B

4   Tommy Docherty

I was a marksman for Manchester United in each of my first four senior matches – against Manchester City, Tottenham Hotspur, Southampton and Wolves. But I was still trying to nail down a regular first-team spot at the end of the season, even though I had become the second-youngest British footballer to win international honours, for with only eight full League games behind me, I had made my debut for Northern Ireland against Spain in a European Nations Cup match switched to Hull because of the troubles in Belfast.

Eight full League matches, half a dozen appearances as substitute, an international within three months of my debut in the First Division . . . but although I was only 17 years and 198 days old when I was capped, things hadn't gone smoothly all the way for me – or for Manchester United.

The slide down the First Division table had brought about a change in management, and Tommy Docherty, formerly the team boss of Scotland, was in charge as I recovered from that car crash. And immediately the transfer rumours began to fly around.

United had signed striker Ted MacDougall from Bournemouth for something like £200,000, and he was unsettled. But The Doc made it clear that United would not be selling 'until such time as we think we can improve our squad.' So, while I was out of action, Ted MacDougall wasn't for sale.

As for my future, it was reassuring to read that Tommy Docherty had said: 'We rate the boy very highly, and we want him back in the squad as soon as possible.' But the fact remained that The Doc had already dropped MacDougall, that there was talk of a near-£200,000 bid by West Ham to take him back south . . . and, above all, there was the knowledge for me that I had not only to prove my match fitness to my own satisfaction, but prove to The Doc by my performances that I deserved to stay at United AND nail down a regular first-team place.

I knew that Tommy Docherty had a reputation for being ruthless when he felt that players should be on their way, that he was always ready to inject new talent into a team, and that he was a man for making up his mind about a player swiftly. Maybe he had already made up his mind about me before I'd got back into action!

Someone once described me as an honest player, with few illusions. Not a bad description, either, though I say it myself. And my experience at Old Trafford had taught me a fair amount – enough, in fact, to be prepared for anything. I'd become an Irish international virtually before I had claimed a regular first-team place, I'd found myself spending week after week as substitute, in the early days of season 1972–73, I'd seen United sitting on top of the table and scrambling to avoid relegation. And the car crash had halted my ideas of clinching that regular place in the senior side.

I used to lie in that hospital bed pondering on what life would be like under The Doc. United had Wyn Davies, Ted MacDougall and Brian Kidd, and it seemed to me that Tommy Docherty would soon be sorting out players and wheeling and dealing in his rumbustious style. I remember lying there and thinking to myself: 'What chance have I got?' And frankly, I felt that once I was fit again, I must be on my way.

The Doc and Paddy Crerand came to see me when I was in hospital, and that was the first time I had ever set eyes on United's controversial manager. We chatted for a while, but never at any time did The Doc assure me that there was a place for me at Old Trafford. When I left hospital I wasn't able to play from the January to the end of the season, when I took part in a youth tournament in Switzerland. The Doc had told me: 'I'm going on the trip, and I will watch you.' So it was crystal-clear that from his point of view, I was on trial.

To be honest, I felt that it was a little bit unfair to pass judgement on me so quickly, and in such a brief space of time, for I was still struggling with my breathing. I think The Doc knew this and took it into account, for at least he dropped a few words of praise in my direction for fighting to get fit for the tour. I played in all the games, although I could tell I wasn't 100 per cent, and at the end of the trip Tommy Docherty had made up his mind about me. He told me : 'I'm keeping you on. I'll give you a chance.' So I owe Tommy Docherty that much.

But while he kept his word to me, I had still known him only a very brief time, and being given a chance and taking it could turn out to be two different things, so far as he was concerned. There was a long way to go before I discovered what the new manager was really like, through day-to-day contact.

I can truthfully say that practically my first experience of Tommy Docherty was when he was taking the mickey out of me – by slipping a 'mickey finn' into my drink. That was while we were on the youth-team trip to Switzerland, and staying in Geneva. I was sitting with Brian Greenhoff in the bar of the hotel when The Doc walked in. He asked me if I would like a drink, and I ordered a couple of lagers, with due thanks to the manager.

The drinks arrived, and I saw that Brian had begun to laugh, so I asked him what was wrong. After I had drunk my lager I was all over the place . . . not surprising, considering that The Doc had added a certain ingredient to my drink when I wasn't looking. Not that I knew it at the time – I was too busy trying to make it to the bedroom and get myself sorted out! Brian told me next morning what had happened.

I got to know Tommy Docherty much better as the months went by, and I came to realise that here was a flamboyant character who was a law unto himself. If he liked you, and you got along together – which usually meant doing things the way The Doc demanded – then all well and good; if you crossed him, then watch out for trouble!

One day we were having a practice match and trying to work out some tactical moves involving the defence, and The

Doc kept on stopping the game to make points. He would keep on blowing the whistle to halt the proceedings and, at one stage, Martin Buchan lost his rag and caustically asked the manager how he expected the players to do what they were supposed to be doing if he kept on blowing the whistle.

There was no messing about, as The Doc gave Martin his marching orders. 'If you don't want to do it, go and get bathed,' he ordered. It's the only time I've seen a player sent off in a practice match.

The Doc got me in lumber with my team-mates during a tour United made to Australia. It started with a straightforward phone call from The Doc to me before we had even left England. He rang to tell me that while we were out there the Australians would be organising a competition and that three United players were wanted to take on three Aussie footballers at volleyball. Furthermore, I would receive £150 for taking part, and the money would be my own.

I was very happy to agree, and thought no more about the matter . . . until the complications started, once we had arrived in Australia. Alex Stepney casually asked me where I was going, one day, and I told him about the competition – Brian Greenhoff and Steve Coppell were also scheduled to take part – and Alex then asked me if I would be paying my money into the players' pool. When I said that so far as I was concerned, the fee being paid was to me, and that it would be my own money, Alex got a bit upset.

The next thing that happened was a players' meeting. By that time, I was feeling a bit upset myself, for I was still only a young player, and I didn't know anything about players' pools. I'd been asked to do a job and been told I was getting paid for it. That had seemed simple enough, at the time. Suddenly, it had become a matter of doing my team-mates down, and I'd never even thought about anything like that. I couldn't see what all the fuss was about.

However, the three of us – Brian, Steve and myself – kept the peace by paying the money we had received into the players' pool, so that was the end of that. But I was in a thoroughly bad mood when the tournament ended, because apart from losing what I considered to be cash I had earned fairly and squarely, I got a telling-off from Tommy Docherty. Nothing to do with the money . . . but he'd been my partner at volleyball, and we'd lost to our Australian opponents. The Doc didn't like that one little bit.

There was another time when The Doc wasn't so pleased – though I wasn't the target for his wrath on that occasion – when the team was returning by coach from a match in the Midlands, and the manager decided to pay a visit to the 'loo' at the rear of the coach. One player who shall remain name-less decided to lock The Doc in, and suddenly the rest of us became aware of a banging and hammering at the back of the coach . . . then the next moment the toilet door was swinging off its hinges and an irate Doc was emerging.

By then, everyone had twigged what had happened, and this didn't improve Tommy Docherty's temper. But the player who suffered for that escapade was little David McCreery, who was the first person Tommy Docherty saw as he stormed out of the toilet. He grabbed David's head, banged it against the window, then marched back to his own seat.

By and large, I got on all right with Tommy Docherty, probably because I'm a quiet guy who doesn't enjoy having verbal stand-up battles. But there were some players who couldn't avoid a personality clash with the manager, because they were cast in the same mould as he was. Lou Macari, for instance, who always gave as good as he got in face-to-face arguments with The Doc – though I must say United's man-ager never seemed to hold a grudge.

The Doc's style tends to be aggressive, and there are only two ways to counter that. You either keep quiet or you blast it out with him. One thing which cannot be argued – Tommy Docherty will make decisions on the spot, whereas most other managers will stop to think – and think again. Sometimes swift decision-making can turn out to be a good thing, other times I think it can rebound. I reckoned the decision to sell Gerry Daly was made in haste and possibly repented at leisure. Certainly I believe he is a good player and should never have been allowed to leave Manchester United.

I suppose that, in a way, I was instrumental in putting a

question mark against the future of Gerry at Old Trafford, for it was when Tommy Docherty signed Jimmy Greenhoff from Stoke that problems began to arise. Obviously, considering that Jimmy had cost around £120,000, he wasn't going to join Manchester United and play in the reserve side, and the fact that he was an out-and-out striker meant something – or, rather, someone – had to give.

Jimmy took my place in the front line . . . and that left three of us – Lou Macari, Gerry Daly and myself – in competition for midfield places. Fortunately for me, I was the first one to be given a chance of nailing down the midfield job, and though Gerry and I remained the best of friends off the field, we were still rivals when it came to being in the first team.

Gerry didn't like losing his place, and he told me he had been to see the manager to have a chat about the situation. 'I'm not having a go at you,' Gerry said to me, 'my complaint is the way The Doc has gone about things.' And that was how the rift between Gerry Daly and the manager who had signed him really began. Apart from being the team's penalty expert – I think he missed only one, against West Brom, during his time at Old Trafford – Gerry had tremendous ability as a creative midfield player, and he had a keen footballing brain. Still has, for that matter. When he steps up for a spot-kick, for instance, he takes a long run and, nine times out of 10, manages to send the goalkeeper the wrong way.

Gerry and Mick Martin arrived from Ireland at around the same time, and both proved bargain buys, for United made a handsome profit on each player when he was transferred. To be honest, I don't think United could ever really decide which was Mick's best position, though he was usually in the reckoning for a midfield role. But he reckoned he was best in a back-four spot, alongside the centre-half, and that's where he wound up at West Brom.

You could be sure of one thing while Tommy Docherty was the manager of Manchester United – he didn't let the grass grow under his feet. There was never a day when you went down to the ground for training without wondering who was coming and who was on his way, for players came and went in quick succession.

Denis Law was given a free transfer, and The Doc sold Ted MacDougall, Wyn Davies, Steve James, Willie Morgan and Brian Kidd. Morgan had been the skipper of Scotland during the time Tommy Docherty was the international team manager, and their relationship certainly deteriorated towards the end of Willie's time at Old Trafford. Brian Kidd, a local lad, had been an idol of the Stretford Enders and was United-daft, and when he took his boots from Old Trafford it must have been one of the worst moments of his life.

There were other players whom The Doc not only bought, but sold . . . Jim McCalliog and Gerry Daly, for instance. He signed George Graham and made him skipper, he signed Alex Forsyth, Lou Macari, Paddy Roche, Jim Holton, Mick Martin, Steve Coppell, Stuart Pearson, Gordon Hill, Ron Davies, Tommy Baldwin, Alan Foggon. Yes, the turnover of playing talent at Manchester United during Tommy Docherty's regime was quite something.

George Graham had my sympathy when he was at Old Trafford, for he had some trouble winning over the fans. He came into the side at a bad time, for relegation was staring United in the face, and though he was made skipper he never seemed to hit it off with the supporters, who gave him some terrible stick at times. George was slow, casual and deliberate – his play was in the style of Paddy Crerand – and perhaps his transfer to Manchester United came too late in his career, for he had been a great footballer, but was coming towards the close of his top-class playing days.

Ted MacDougall was never really long enough at Old Trafford to convince people of his ability, and possibly here was an example of someone being destroyed by a big price tag, for he had cost Manchester United £200,000 when he was signed from Bournemouth, and he was expected to live up to his reputation as a marksman – people didn't forget that he had once hammered in nine goals in a Cup-tie, for instance, though that was for Bournemouth and against non-League opposition, in Margate.

Frank O'Farrell had signed Ted . . . and it was The Doc who quickly decided that the striker should be on his way. MacDougall hadn't scored many goals for United, but I felt that the decision to let him go was a bit swift, because the lad himself could probably have claimed he never really had the chance to show what he could do, since his stay was relatively brief.

The list of players who crossed swords with The Doc at Manchester United is considerable – MacDougall, Martin Buchan, Lou Macari, Gerry Daly, Jim Holton, Willie Morgan, Tony Young, Alex Stepney . . . and Alex, perhaps, was the one man who made Tommy Docherty hold up his hand, for he was dropped, then came back to give United a lot more first-team service before moving into American Soccer.

Tommy Docherty's decision to drop Alex and promote Paddy Roche rebounded in two ways, for apart from having to admit later that he had been wrong in his assessment that Stepney's first-team days were numbered, the effect on Paddy's career was somewhat traumatic, for the publicity which followed, as United conceded goals during Paddy's short spell in the senior side at that time, all but destroyed him. Paddy took an awful lot of stick, and the experience clearly did him a great deal of harm.

Alex Stepney took it hard when he found he was being axed, and he didn't mince his words when he said : 'I'll back my judgment against that of Tommy Docherty'. And in the end, The Doc had to confess that Alex had proved his point. He went on to regain a first-team place, and by the time Dave Sexton had arrived at Old Trafford Alex Stepney had taken his total of appearances in the League alone to 550, with more than 400 of those games in goal for Manchester United. That gave him an average of more than 30 League matches a season in a dozen terms at Old Trafford – and he added to his impressive total before bowing out.

Paddy Roche faced two of the most difficult matches possible, when The Doc thrust him into sudden prominence with the shock announcement about the dropping of Alex Stepney, for United were due to play Liverpool and Manchester City, in quick succession. I feel that the sudden limelight didn't help his nerves, and when the goals started going in against us, he was on a hiding to nothing.

A goalkeeper needs to make only one mistake, and people

don't let him forget it. Paddy himself admitted that he did make some errors, and straight away, the ammunition was there for the critics. There was one occasion at Old Trafford when a team-mate passed the ball back to Paddy and, as he collected it, there came from the crowd an audible sigh of relief. It was deliberately affected, of course, but it emphasised the pressures on the newcomer in goal.

The worst of it is that when a 'keeper is seen to be nervous, the defenders in front of him tend to develop nerves, as well, and in such a situation it is inevitable that more mistakes are made, as people become hesitant. And in Paddy's defence it has to be said that team-mates made mistakes . . . but when the ball goes into the net, people tend to put it all down to the man between the posts.

One player who caused more controversy than most during his stay at Old Trafford was Gordon Hill, the winger signed by Tommy Docherty from Millwall. Gordon scored some magnificent goals – he could volley a ball from any height, and the best goal I ever saw him score was one against Sheffield Wednesday, when he took on and beat four men, then slipped the ball round the 'keeper.

In the 1976 F.A. Cup semi-final against Derby County, he struck both United's goals and finished as the hero of the day, so far as United's fans were concerned. One goal, from a free-kick outside the 18-yard box, went in with the help of a slight deflection, while the other was a left-footer, on the volley, from 25 yards. Gordon could certainly belt the ball on the volley, and I find it easy to believe the story the lads told of an occasion when we were playing away from home and, the night before the game, Gordon had his room-mate, Steve Paterson, throwing toilet rolls to him so that he could practise volleying and landing them on the bed.

Yes, spectacular goals have been Gordon's stock-in-trade; but towards the end of his time at Manchester United his style of play produced increasing controversy, with the argument being that though his goals were often scored in a sensational manner, he didn't contribute as much as he might have done towards the all-round teamwork.

My view of him? – I felt that he wasn't essentially a team

man – but you could more or less count on him getting 20 goals a season. He was a good player to have in the side when things were going well – no doubt about that – because he could demolish and demoralise the opposition; but when the chips were down and you needed solid grafting, you had to look to other members of the side to provide more than their share of it.

Gordon was an exciting player, and I was often able to admire his skill and the panache he brought to his game, but there were occasions when you looked at what he was doing – often he seemed to be going it alone – and you felt an increasing sense of frustration, because he wasn't getting anywhere. There was a memorable occasion when he received a cuff on the head from Martin Buchan during a match, and that should give you some idea of what I mean by frustration. And I don't really think there could be any in-between . . . you were either a Gordon Hill fan, or you weren't.

Certainly he won over the Stretford Enders with the flair he could display, and the breathtaking goals he could score, and there always seemed to be a buzz of excitement when he pounced on a pass. But I felt he was a loner, on and off the field, and sometimes I got the impression that he felt a bit out of it in the north, and was missing the familiar sights and sounds of London.

Yet he had a chirpy, bouncy personality and a lively sense of humour, and when he was taken to task and told he was required to graft more for the team, rather than rely upon individual touches of brilliance, he would answer back with the question : 'What do you want me to do – score 20 goals or none at all?'

Gordon finally went to play for The Doc again, at Derby, and United signed another left-sided player, Mickey Thomas, from Wrexham. He was one of manager Dave Sexton's recruits, and I don't think anyone would dispute that while Mickey may not find the target as regularly as Gordon did, his work rate is at least twice as high. Mickey is a team man and one of the game's workers – which is how I like to think of myself – and I believe now that the fans, while not forgetting the brilliant touches which Gordon could produce when he was on song, have taken the Welsh lad to their hearts just as much as they admired Gordon. Which is quite a tribute to Mickey, for it's a big job not only to take over someone else's jersey, but his fan club as well.

Manchester United have never been backward in spending huge fees, when they felt there was a player available who could add something to the team, and Mickey Thomas cost around £330,000. But a player who does command a big fee also has to justify it in the eyes of the supporters, as well as his team-mates. And to be blunt, if he comes off, I think he is idolised more than a player who grew up at the club and cost nothing.

Despite that 'George Best' label which was pinned on me in the early days, I have never kidded myself that I'm one of football's glamour boys. To me, it has always been the case that the star who cost a massive fee is the one the fans will cheer most . . . providing he produces the goods. But if he's a flop, the price tag and the reputation this carries will rebound on him.

I've always felt that I have got on well with the United supporters, without being one of the glamour boys – but I know there are players in the team whom the fans cheer more than myself. Maybe it's because such players appear to be more flamboyant or score more goals, or cost a high fee, while the one who cost nothing is regarded as just another member of the side. But I can honestly say that the only reason I've sometimes wished I had cost a million pounds is because of the signing-on fee I would have received!

5 Season of Decision

Season 1973–74 was one of decision – for myself, and (as it turned out) for Manchester United. I had got over the car crash, made a comeback by playing in the youth tournament in Switzerland, and was set on claiming a regular first-team place at the earliest possible moment. But Tommy Docherty decided that on kick-off day the place for me was the substitute's bench. So I sat and watched as Manchester United conceded three goals against Arsenal at Highbury.

Gerry Daly was the player who made way for me in the next match, and we beat Stoke City 1–0 at Old Trafford, then scored a 2–1 win against Queen's Park Rangers on home ground. Our first goal came when I took a corner kick and Jim Holton knocked the ball home, and I was the one who hit the winner. We played two more matches and lost them, and I was dropped from the team. I couldn't grumble, either, because I knew that while I had been trying my hardest, I didn't feel 100 per cent. I had to admit to myself that probably I had been too eager to return to action after the crash, and the result was that, because my fitness was still suspect, my form had suffered.

It took me several more months to achieve the kind of fitness I knew was required, if I were to become recognised as a regular in First Division football, and I did it by pacing myself through a fair number of reserve-team matches, with the result that I did not return to the first team until towards the end of 1973. And by then, the battle to escape the drop to the Second Division was on with a vengeance, even though there was still half the campaign to go.

United had been living a kind of Jekyll-and-Hyde existence, for while we had drawn against the likes of Liverpool and Leeds (at Elland Road), we had lost at home to Derby County, dropped points at Old Trafford against Chelsea, Norwich and Southampton, and suffered a 3–2 defeat on our own ground at the hands of Coventry. So this meant that we had – in our view, at any rate – thrown away seven precious points.

When we lost 2–0 to Liverpool at Anfield towards the end of December, we had taken only one point out of a possible seven that month, and the relegation writing was really on the wall, for Manchester United, the glamour club of English football, were separated from the bottom place in the First Division by only three clubs . . . Birmingham, Norwich City and West Ham.

At that stage of the game, the Hammers looked to be in dire trouble, for they had taken only 11 points from their 21 matches, while United, Birmingham and Norwich, each with a game in hand, were only a point or two better off. Three of the bottom four clubs – United, Birmingham and Norwich – had failed to win even one match on away grounds, and we had lost seven games out of nine on tour, while our slips at home meant that we had won four, drawn four and lost three of our outings at Old Trafford.

The last Saturday of the year brought a glimmer of renewed hope for us, because while we were beating Ipswich 2–0 at Old Trafford, other teams in trouble were losing or sharing the points on home grounds. Birmingham could only draw, 1–1, against Leeds at St Andrew's; West Ham went down 2–0 against Spurs at White Hart Lane; and Norwich finished with a 1–1 draw against Manchester City at Carrow Road.

We left it a bit late to produce the pay-off punch against Ipswich, for play had been going for almost 80 minutes before I managed to stick the ball in the net, and two minutes later Lou Macari scored to make the margin more decisive. Ironically, it was Denis Law – playing for Manchester City – who robbed Norwich of a win with his equaliser at Carrow Road, while the man who got the Canaries' goal was another former Manchester United striker, Ted MacDougall. And believe it or not, but the long arm of Soccer coincidence that day was stretched even further, because the marksman for Leeds in the 1–1 draw at Birmingham was Joe Jordan, who later cost Manchester United £350,000.

For us, the results generally made good reading that day, and we could feel pleased that we had beaten an Ipswich side which was high up the First Division table. Yet, like the 36,000 people who had watched our match, we went home pondering what the second half of the season held in store, though we had opened up a bit of a points gap, for Norwich and West Ham were bracketed on the bottom, with 13 apiece, while Birmingham and ourselves then had 16 points, which meant we were not too far behind Chelsea (18) and Wolves and Stoke (19 each).

Frankly, I knew I was still struggling to stay the pace of a game for 90 minutes, although I was back in United's side, and the fact that the team as a whole was finding the going hard didn't help any, either. Denis Law had faded from the Old Trafford scene, after his controversial free transfer, Brian Kidd had travelled south to play for Arsenal – a move which did not receive unanimous approval from a considerable number of the fans at Old Trafford – and George Best, it seemed, had finally carried out his intention to quit.

All the wheeling and dealing had meant quite a lot of chopping and changing in the team, and I wasn't the only one to find the road a bit rocky, for Lou Macari, who had cost United £200,000 when he was transferred from Glasgow Celtic, wasn't making the impact that people had expected from a player of his reputation.

Originally, Liverpool had been first in the field for Lou's signature, and it seemed almost cut and dried when he travelled to Anfield for discussions with Bill Shankly. Liverpool were playing a game that night, and Lou was closeted with their manager after the match . . . but within 48 hours, he had become a Manchester United player. However, as time went on, he didn't need anyone to tell him that his critics were saying it would have been better for United if he'd joined Liverpool.

I felt sorry for Lou, because I realised just how hard he was trying to show that he was really a class player – at that time, the trouble was that he simply hadn't found his best position in the side, for he started off in the front line, and it was only when he began to develop a deeper role that he finally clicked.

I felt sorry, too, for Ian Moore, who was hampered so much by injury, and it was a bitter blow to player and club when this tremendously talented winger was lost to the game.

It's always a tragedy when a professional footballer has to hang up his boots because an injury has curtailed his career, but United certainly felt the loss of Ian Moore, who had been a £200,000 investment from Nottingham Forest. Derby County had been in for him originally, and it seemed at one time that United had missed the boat, for County's manager at the time, Brian Clough, had even paraded Ian at the Baseball Ground as a Derby signing . . . but in the end, United were back in the hunt and they got their man.

However, fortune didn't smile upon Ian or his new club. And he could have become rated as a truly great player with a flair for scoring goals. He had a tremendous amount of skill, and possessed a lot of pace, and it was a terrible blow when he received the injury which was to put an end to his top-class career. He had quickly become a firm favourite with the Old Trafford faithful, but really he didn't have long enough to achieve what he had initially promised, because of the injury, though he made a brave fight of it. The latter part of his time at United saw him in and out of the side, and he had to keep on visiting the specialists to check on his ankle injury.

Law, Kidd, Best, Moore . . . four of the finest forwards in the business. And Manchester United certainly missed them. United also missed the goals they could have scored for the club, for this was one department in which we were lacking. We lost 3–0 away to Queen's Park Rangers on the first day of January, 1974, and that defeat pushed us to third from the bottom; furthermore, only Norwich (17) had scored fewer goals than United (20), while 10 teams had conceded more than the 30 which opponents had stuck past us. With hindsight, it is possible to make some kind of judgment, and later on we realised that, for one thing, we had been trying to play too defensively – a trait which had never been part of United's make-up.

The F.A. Cup brought us a bit of relief as we defeated Plymouth Argyle in the third round at Old Trafford – but it took a goal from Lou Macari after more than an hour's play to settle that game against a side from the Third Division, and it was possible to tell from the gate of just over 31,000 that our fans were beginning to lose their faith in us.

I scored in our next League match, at West Ham, but goals from Billy Bonds and Pat Holland brought their team a victory in a match which was worth four points to the winners, since the Hammers were also at the wrong end of the First Division. That defeat pushed us into 21st place, and the writing was on the wall.

We had to rely on a goal from defender Steve James to give us a point from our home game against Arsenal, and Ipswich Town returned to Old Trafford towards the end of January to inflict a 1–0 defeat on us and knock us out of the F.A. Cup. Kevin Beattie did the damage, after only seven minutes, and 37,000 fans didn't enjoy the rest of the match, as we laboured in vain to salvage a replay.

It was Coventry City 1, Manchester United 0, and when we met Leeds at Old Trafford they scored twice, through Mick Jones and Joe Jordan, while we couldn't even stick one goal past them. There were more than 60,000 spectators at the match . . . and that result sent us to the foot of the First Division, with only 17 points from 27 games. Even Norwich were a point better off than United.

Goals from Brian Greenhoff and Stewart Houston enabled us to snatch a 2–2 draw at Derby, in a fighting display after we had gone two down in half an hour, but we failed to find the net against Wolves at Old Trafford, and dropped a home point.

Hopes were revived when we went to Bramall Lane and Lou Macari scored a goal which turned out to be the winner against Sheffield United, but when we went to St Andrew's, a Joe Gallagher goal three minutes from time ended our hopes of pinching a point against Birmingham, and with only 10 matches to go, we still occupied 21st place in the First Division.

There was going to be no easy way out, either, for Norwich (on the bottom) had 21 points, so they were just one behind us, while Birmingham's victory meant that they had put three points between ourselves and them, even though they lay directly above us in the table. And the next club above them, Southampton, had 29 points . . . which left us seven adrift, and knowing that three clubs were destined to make the drop.

Tottenham Hotspur travelled to Manchester and scored a 1–0 win, courtesy of a Ralph Coates goal, then we went to Carrow Road and scored a surprise, 2–0 win over Norwich, with goals from Brian Greenhoff and Lou Macari. Jim McCalliog, another of Tommy Docherty's signings, hit the lone goal which won our home game against Newcastle, and with five matches to the finishing line it was still touch and go, for we had pulled up to within three points of South-ampton (still fourth from bottom), were two points behind Birmingham, and led Norwich by four points. They were as good as down, so that meant there were probably three clubs struggling to avoid the last two places, for Newcastle – on 34 points – looked like being safe.

A penalty goal from Jim McCalliog in the desperate fight for survival earned us a point at Southampton, and we had three matches to go . . . while the Saints and Birmingham had two apiece left, though we were still a point behind Birming-ham and two adrift of the Saints. By then, Newcastle were half-way up the table, and West Ham, immediately above Southampton, were on 36 points and had just one game to play.

The end of the season brought a dramatic match at Old Trafford against our arch-rivals, Manchester City . . . and Denis Law, who was in the City line-up, turned out to be the central character. It was a game we desperately needed to win – or so it seemed, at the time – and the last 10 minutes of the match arrived with the scoreline still reading 0–0.

Eight minutes from what was scheduled to be the final whistle, Denis got the ball into our net – and there was pandemonium, as the fans erupted and spilled over on to the pitch. It became clear that there was no way the game could be completed with personal safety assured, and four minutes after the goal, the teams were told the game had been abandoned.

On the same day, Southampton had gone to Goodison Park, taken on an Everton side which stood high up the First Division table, and staggered football by scoring a resounding, 3–0 victory with goals from Peter Osgood, Mike Channon and Brian O'Neill. But that result wasn't enough to save the Saints from taking the drop along with Norwich, whose fate was already assured.

The Canaries had 29 points, with one match to play; United had 32 points from 40 games; Southampton had 36 points and had completed their programme. But the one which counted wasn't the Denis Law goal . . . it was the result at St Andrew's, where Birmingham had beaten Norwich 2–1, with goals from Bob Hatton and Kenny Burns. That meant Birmingham had completed their fixtures, too – but they had wound up with 37 points. There was no way Manchester United could catch them. And we finished the season still on the 32-point mark, which meant we were down. We had scored only 35 goals in 42 League matches . . . and I finished as the club's leading First Division marksman. My tally? – Just half a dozen goals!

So United faced a future in the Second Division – something which had seemed unthinkable in the not-so-distant past –and I personally wondered if my future would be in Second Division football, or if I would be 'on my bike'. The Doc had been fair to me, but six League goals were not exactly a passport to success, even if they made me the leading scorer in the side.

I know now, looking back, that not only had I been plagued by the after-effects of the car crash and affected by playing in a struggling side; I had been worrying all the time as to whether or not my style of play was suiting The Doc. I decided there and then that if he kept me at Old Trafford, I wasn't going to do myself any good unless I stopped worrying about what other people thought, and concentrated on playing as well as I knew how. Yes, even if I did make some mistakes.

If we were feeling gloomy about our descent to the Second Division, it became clear that no-one was more down about it than The Doc. And he worked out a new strategy for the team as United made their bid to bounce back to the top flight at the first time of asking. The defensive formula which seemed to have weighed us down during season 1973-74 was banished . . . the accent was to be on attack, attack. We would revert to the recognised Manchester United style of play, going for goals, entertaining, and believing that the results would come.

It was a policy which paid off handsomely during the next campaign, for we hammered teams out of sight, and proved to be the biggest shot in the arm the Second Division had ever known. Now that I've played in both divisions, I can assess the difference between the two – and I'll say straight away that if it's difficult when you're struggling to stay in the First, it can be a damned sight harder trying to climb out of the Second. Especially if you are Manchester United.

There are so many better players in the First Division, and so many teams in the Second which rely on organisation to make up for the shortage in skill. The result is that Second Division sides generally are tough nuts to crack. I still maintain that Manchester United did remarkably well to bounce straight back as champions of the Second Division, because so many of the things we encountered during our season in Division 2 were strange to us.

There were the compact grounds as Brisbane Road, Boundary Park and The Den, where the fans are virtually breathing down your neck. I remember playing Oldham at Boundary Park, and they beat us 1–0 – though, by rights, the scoreline should have read 2–0. They were on the attack, and Oldham's Ronnie Blair – a Northern Ireland-international team-mate of mine – was in midfield when the ball was crossed from the right. He caught the ball in mid-air with the side of his foot and the shot zipped into the net, hit a stanchion and came out again. It happened so quickly that the referee was under the impression the ball had hit the bar, and he waved play on. But it should have been a goal, all right.

To be blunt, none of us looked forward to visiting some of the outposts of the League's Soccer empire, after regular trips to places like Anfield, Goodison Park, Highbury and White

Hart Lane. We knew, further, that once United's relegation fears had been confirmed, not only were people talking about us – many of them were saying this was the worst side United had had for years, and that there was a crying need for new players (though United HAD done a fair amount of wheeling and dealing before relegation).

However, there had been a glimmer of light towards the end of the season, because we had started to push forward and carry the attack to the opposition. It had come too late to salvage First Division status, but it determined our thinking for the promotion campaign.

They say that self-examination is good for the soul, and during the final stages of our retreat from the First Division, everyone at Old Trafford did a great deal of heart-searching. It was, as someone at the club had observed, unthinkable that Manchester United should be condemned to second-class status, but in our heart of hearts, we knew that we simply hadn't shown the form everyone expected from a club which was so rich in tradition.

The days of glory, clearly, belonged to the past, and it was going to take a lot of sheer hard work to restore the tarnished image. We might feel that it was rough justice, we certainly were a bit bewildered by our fall from grace. But to me, at any rate, there was no blinking the facts. United were down – and, in my book, that meant we had hit rock-bottom.

6 'What Are We Doing Here?'

More than once, during the season Manchester United were sentenced to Second Division football, we went out asking ourselves what we were doing there. It was an experience, all right – and, sometimes, an education. Because if we didn't exactly welcome our drop in status, the teams and fans waiting for us in Division 2 were not only pleased to see us . . . in many cases they were out to do us. And all because of two little words – Manchester United.

United's record and reputation through the years made it inevitable that our fall from First Division grace was savoured by a lot of people. I won't say they were sadistic about it, but they certainly enjoyed seeing us taken down a peg. And it was natural that teams who found themselves doing battle with the fallen giants were all out to show that they could match us. More than that, they often went out with the idea that if they couldn't compete against us when it came to sheer skill, they could give us a lesson when it came to the physical side of football. So we took some stick.

The pulling power of Manchester United was reflected in the gates everywhere we played, and fears that our descent into the Second Division would damage our attendance figures were dispelled. Indeed, for four successive seasons, including the one we were in the second grade, United's home gates topped the million mark, while crowds were well above average when we played away from Old Trafford.

Some people have said that a season in the Second Division was good for me, personally, because it toughened me up. I can only say that I enjoyed my term in Division 2 . . . I would have enjoyed playing in the Fourth Division, come to that, because for me it meant that I was able to resume my career after the car crash which, I had feared for a time, might mean the end of League football.

I vividly remember some of the matches we played that season – there was one ground, which shall be nameless, where the fans spat at us as we walked out for the match. There was the game at York City's Bootham Crescent ground, where the opposition did their best – and failed – to provide their manager, Wilf McGuinness, with a victory. Wilf, of course, must have had mixed emotions about this meeting, when he thought of his days in charge at Old Trafford.

The games against Aston Villa and Bristol City were hard-fought affairs, though we all celebrated in the end by claiming promotion and we found it hard going at Meadow Lane, when we met Notts County, at Oldham, and at Roker Park, where I was very impressed by the ground, the atmosphere, and the support which the home fans gave to Sunderland.

Our first game in the Second Division was against Orient at Brisbane Road, and there was a crowd of just under 18,000. Even though gates had gone down during the previous season, we had still been used to playing in front of double that number at Old Trafford, and there had been times when we had pulled in more than 60,000 people. The atmosphere was lacking – but it was the result that mattered.

We knew better than anybody that the critics would be looking first to see how Manchester United had fared that Saturday in August, and a lot of people had the idea that we might fall flat on our faces. I won't deny that there was some apprehension among us as we walked out on the Brisbane Road pitch, but Willie Morgan helped to settle us when he scored after 26 minutes, and we hung on to that slender lead until there were fewer than 20 minutes to go. Then Stewart Houston got his name on the scoresheet, and we were home and dry.

The gate at Old Trafford for our game against Millwall was better than any other that day, apart from the one at Anfield; almost 42,000 fans, heartened by our initial victory, came to cheer us on to another . . . and we obliged by hammering Millwall 4–0. The first goal came after only three minutes, and it was scored by Stuart Pearson, who had been signed from Hull in a £200,000 deal. A tremendous start for Stuart, and a tonic for United, who found the fans were cheering them every minute after that.

Gerry Daly set the seal on things by scoring a hat-trick which included two penalty goals, and the pattern was set for the remainder of the season. We pulled in the fans at Old Trafford, and wherever else we played we boosted gates in the Second Division. We also maintained our winning ways as we attacked, attacked, attacked.

I was playing up front for United, and I found myself up against some big fellows – defenders like Brian Stubbs and Dave Needham, then with Notts County, Gary Collier, who played for Bristol City, and Barry Kitchener, of Millwall. These tough-as-teak players were hard, but fair . . . there were others who seemed to have the idea that it was good tactics to put the boot in first, then think about playing football.

Fulham had former England stars Bobby Moore and Alan Mullery playing for them, Laurie Cunningham was still making his way with Orient, Paul Hart was with Blackpool, a former United team-mate, Mick Martin, was playing for West Brom, and in Villa's Second Division side there was talent such as Brian Little and John Gidman.

We made our best start for years, when we ran up four wins in successive matches, but if we had any thoughts that it was going to be a stroll back to the First Division such notions were soon dispelled as the road became harder. Before we played Nottingham Forest at Old Trafford, we were given good-luck symbols – believe it or not, horses' tails – by a beaming fan from Ghana who (naturally) wore a shirt which was the same red as our Manchester United jerseys.

But we needed to inject a lot of sheer, hard work into our play to wind up with a point against a team which contested every inch of ground. Only the previous week, the Forest players had been given a verbal roasting by their manager at the time, Allan Brown, who had accused some of his players of cheating in their attitude.

Forest's attitude at Old Trafford certainly left no room for doubts : they had come determined to show everyone what they could do, and they went close to beating us.

We found ourselves a goal down for the first time that

season, after having begun as if we would give Forest the
runaround. We scored first, through Brian Greenhoff, then
Forest rapped back with goals from Ian Bowyer and John
Cottam, and we just managed to sneak an equaliser, when I
tucked away a chance 10 minutes from time.

Generally speaking, though, we were on a winning streak
right through the season, even if we had one or two ups and
downs. A Pearson goal earned us a point at West Brom, we
beat Bristol Rovers 2–0, and though we lost 2–0 at Norwich,
after 10 matches we had picked up 16 points and were sitting
on top of the table, three points ahead of the Canaries, who
were our nearest challengers.

Two Pearson goals won the game at Fulham, I chipped in
with a goal against Notts County at Old Trafford, and goals
by Alex Forsyth, Lou Macari and Jim McCalliog shattered
Blackpool at Bloomfield Road. More than 48,000 spectators
saw another Pearson goal do the trick at Old Trafford against
Southampton, and 25 points from 15 games told the story of
a rejuvenated Manchester United, as we led the field by four
points.

It was a Pearson hat-trick and a Macari solo that demo-
lished Oxford at Old Trafford, and we shrugged off a 1–0
defeat at Bristol City by beating Aston Villa 2–1 on our own
ground, thanks to Gerry Daly. He hit both goals, one of them
from the penalty spot. So we were six points in front, with
29 from 18 matches, and we arrived at the half-way mark of
the season by beating Sunderland at Old Trafford and sharing
eight goals with Sheffield Wednesday in a thriller at Hillsborough. Players and fans alike had to have strong hearts as
these ding-dong matches swung first one way, then the other!

When Sunderland turned up at Old Trafford for the League
confrontation, they had lost only two matches in the previous
16 months, while we had been at the top of the Second
Division since the start of the season, so there was a lot at
stake, in terms of points and prestige, for both teams. It proved
to be one of the most fiercely competitive games in which I
have ever played, and I wasn't the only one left breathless,
at the finish. The 60,000 fans had shouted and cheered themselves hoarse, while all 22 players were whacked.

Sunderland really put us on the rack, as Nottingham Forest had done early in the season. It looked good for us when Stuart Pearson scored with the game only 11 minutes old, but inside the next five minutes the men from Roker Park were the ones with their tails up, for Billy Hughes had turned the scoreline to 2–1 in Sunderland's favour, as he beat Alex Stepney in the 12th and 14th minutes.

We went in at half-time still trailing, but we came out determined to atone for our lapses, and 10 minutes into the second half Willie Morgan got his name on the scoresheet, then – just on the hour – I hit the goal which, as it transpired, produced a 3–2 victory for us, though it was a close thing right to the end.

There were more than 35,000 fans when we went to Hillsborough and tangled with Sheffild Wednesday, and it seemed that Stewart Houston was setting us up for another win when he scored with the game only seven minutes old. But, just as Sunderland had done, Wednesday battled back, and by half-time they were leading 3-1. Lou Macari and Stuart Pearson levelled the scores, then – for the second time in the game – Dave Sunley was on target for Wednesday, to make it 4–3 . . . and nine minutes from time I popped up to hit the final goal and bring United level once more. After such great entertainment, it wasn't surprising that the fans applauded both sides off the park.

Another thriller was the game in which we came up against Charlton (in the League Cup). We gave away a goal in the second minute of the game at Old Trafford – and hit back to score five goals. Charlton, who were third in the Third Division table, hadn't been beaten until they tangled with us, and their goal was the spur we needed. I scored an equaliser within five minutes of the Charlton goal, Phil Warman put through his own goal, and Lou Macari made it 3–1 before half-time. Two more goals in the second half made the scoreline completely decisive.

But there were times when goals were hard to come by, and teams which came to Old Trafford intent on only one thing – stopping us from scoring. Orient did just that, when they played on our ground just before the Christmas. And there was only one goal in another game we desperately wanted to win – fortunately, United were the team which scored it. That was when Manchester City, lording it in the First Division, made the short trip to Old Trafford for a third-round League Cup-tie . . . and the sparks certainly flew. More than 55,000 people turned up at Old Trafford to see if we could knock City off the Wembley trail, and it was hammer and tongs right through the 90 minutes.

Rodney Marsh was playing for City then, and he turned on a fine display of football – twice he got the ball into our net, but each time a goal was disallowed for offside. Early on, also, he combined with Mike Summerbee in a move which ended with the City winger powering a drive which Alex Stepney couldn't hold, and when the rebound went to Dennis Tueart, he sent in a header which was turned for a corner – via a post – by Arthur Albiston.

A few minutes later it was our turn, and Alex Forsyth hammered in a 30-yard shot which City's 'keeper, Keith MacRae, found too hot to handle. The ball thudded against his chest, bounced out of his grasp – and, with Stuart Pearson ready to pounce, MacRae hurriedly booted the ball away.

City came again, and Mike Doyle's 25-yard piledriver zipped past a post, then there was almost one of those freak goals you sometimes see, when City's 'keeper thumped the ball out from the edge of the area . . . and found himself scrambling back to retrieve it, as Jim McCalliog volleyed an immediate return. MacRae palmed away a drive from me which I had thought certain to register on target, then from eight yards or less City's defenders desperately blocked efforts from myself, Lou Macari and Jim McCalliog.

We had a scare when Dennis Tueart hammered in a shot which Alex Stepney couldn't gather cleanly, but the City winger just failed to get another touch to the ball, and it looked odds on a stalemate when, with only 12 minutes of the match remaining, we got the break we had been seeking.

Left-back Arthur Albiston made a run down the flank and curled over a cross which Lou Macari turned inside . . . and City defender Jeff Clarke instinctively handled. Gerry Daly, our spot-kick specialist, put the ball down on the white mark at the Stretford End, and you could have heard a pin drop as he turned, then ran up and placed the ball past the City 'keeper. That's a game Gerry isn't likely to forget, because it was his debut in a derby match.

In the League, we trounced Sheffield United as we hit five goals against them at Old Trafford – I scored the last one with a minute to go, and the United faithful seized on the opportunity to have a laugh at Tony Currie's expense, as they chanted : 'Currie, Currie, what's the score?'

Gates of 40,000-plus were common at Old Trafford – there were 46,000 there to see us take on Notts County a few days after we had sent Manchester City packing from the League Cup, though I have to admit that this was one occasion when we didn't sparkle. I scored the goal that beat County but, to their credit, they refused to be overawed by their surroundings and the atmosphere, and they made us fight all the way.

It seemed that many teams became unsettled when they found themselves playing in front of a crowd two or three times bigger than they were accustomed to, and in one way this was great for us, because we were used to the roar of the faithful at Old Trafford. In another way, I think it probably put even greater pressure on United's players to produce the goods . . . and this was why, sometimes, we failed to live up to the expectations of our fans.

All too often, as well, apart from the knowledge that our supporters came expecting us to win, we were aware that the opposition had arrived with the sole objective of not losing, and when you get this kind of situation, it's always twice as difficult to break down a side which funnels back in defence. As time went on, some of the United players, including myself, even began to prefer playing on other grounds, for as we obeyed Tommy Docherty's instructions to go at teams, we found it was much easier to do this away from home, since our opponents then had to venture out in a bid to create scoring chances themselves. They dare not play a purely defensive role in front of their own supporters – even if the United fans were massed round one side of the ground, as well.

That 4–4 draw at Hillsborough put us on 32 points from 21 matches, so we still had a five-point lead over Sunderland, but the F.A. Cup came as a douche of cold water, as we failed to master Walsall in the third round at Old Trafford, then lost the replay.

However, we met and beat Sheffield Wednesday (2–0) in the return League game, drew no-score at Sunderland (in front of a crowd of almost 46,000) . . . and lost, 1–0, at home against Bristol City. By then, though, we had 40 points from 28 matches and we knew that it would take quite a few accidents to upset our promotion applecart, especially since we still held that five-point lead over Sunderland and were seven points ahead of third-placed Norwich City.

However, when we went to Oxford and lost 1–0, some people began to question whether we were running out of steam, and though we beat Hull the query was being put again, after a 2–0 defeat at Villa Park. We answered the doubters in the best possible way, by hammering Cardiff 4–0 at Old Trafford, and when we travelled the short distance to Burnden Park, we beat Bolton 1–0.

By that time, there were nine matches to go and we had 46 points in the bag. We still had that five-point lead, and a 1–1 home draw against Norwich was followed by a 1–0 victory away against Nottingham Forest. We took our points tally to 52 by beating York 2–1 at Old Trafford, and when a Lou Macari goal at Southampton proved to be the winner on Saturday, April 5, 1975, it was all over, bar the shouting. We had 56 points, and promotion was a certainty.

Sunderland could total only 55, if they won their last three matches, and while Aston Villa could overtake us for the Second Division championship, Norwich needed to win their five remaining games – a tall order, indeed – to equal our total of points to date. And even then, we had a superior goal average. By the time we beat Fulham 1–0 at Old Trafford, it meant we had 58 points and could muster a final tally of 62.

A 2–2 draw against Notts County at Meadow Lane put paid to that idea, but nothing could mar the occasion when we walked out on the Old Trafford pitch for our final home game – against Blackpool – and in front of 58,769 spectators who had come to join in the celebrations, we turned on a performance worthy of divisional champions. Stuart Pearson struck two first-half goals, Lou Macari and Brian Greenhoff made the scoreline 4–0. And for me, it marked the end of a personal battle, because I had spent three years striving to become recognised as an established, first-team player.

It's not too much to say that the Second Division helped to make me – and, for that matter, Stuart Pearson, for together we formed a good combination. He had totalled 17 League goals, I had contributed seven . . . but, more important, I had played in 41 matches and profited from a generous boost in confidence.

The Doc had done his bit by giving me a chance in the side, after the car crash, and he had helped me again by giving me every encouragement to take people on, especially inside the box. 'Don't you worry if you lose the ball occasionally,' he used to tell me. So I profited from that advice, and I believe that Stuart and I helped each other to mature as players.

As for Manchester United, they had done what people had asked of them – bounced back to the top flight at the first time of asking – even though we all knew that the critics would now be wanting to know if we could put it all together in the First Division. It seemed that whether we were doing badly or well, the pressure was never allowed to ease up, for there was always some demand, some challenge, once you had scaled a particular peak.

The mere fact of being Manchester United made the job of winning promotion much more difficult than for any other team, in my view, and I believe it is to the credit of the team that we achieved our objective in such scintillating style. I also think that our supporters deserve a massive vote of thanks for the way they backed us when we were down, and for the way they have continued to follow and encourage us.

There are Manchester United supporters in just about every corner of the world, and no matter where we play, our fans make us aware of their presence. Sometimes some of them step out of line, and it is embarrassing for the team and the club; but in the main most of the people who sport the favours of Manchester United are simply dedicated fans, and not ruffians.

Many people have tried to fathom out the secret of Manchester United's charisma through the years, and my own feeling is that Matt Busby was the man who first gave the club a real identity, for under his guidance, successive teams pursued a policy of entertaining football which also produced results. As the last of the original Busby Babes, I think I can claim to know something about what makes this great club tick, and from my own experience I can easily see how people have come to associate themselves with United.

I wasn't born a Mancunian, although I consider myself one by adoption, after 10 years at the club. But in my days as a schoolboy in Belfast there seemed to me to be a special kind of magic woven around the name of Manchester United. The team had flair and style; the club thought big; the accent was on playing the game in a manner which would entice people to come and cheer; and United were, of course, among the pioneers when it came to competing in Europe.

I was Manchester United-orientated even before George Best had emerged as a star in the Old Trafford firmament. Naturally, once he had arrived, I quickly found someone with whom to identify, and this increased my allegiance to Manchester United. But not every young hopeful had a hero from his own doorstep at Old Trafford.

It seems to me that Matt Busby brought something different to the game, in the way he managed a football club. And in his quest for success there was an air of excitement and adventure. More than that, during his days at the helm, football fans were introduced to so many great talents . . . there was the era of Johnny Carey, Henry Cockburn, Stan Pearson, Jimmy Delaney, Charlie Mitten and Jack Rowley; then came the pre-Munich side; and right the way through, the accent was on attracting the finest possible talent to Old Trafford.

As I was coming up to school-leaving age, I thrilled to the spectacle of Best, Bobby Charlton, Paddy Crerand and Denis Law, and for me, players like these provided the sort of football which made the blood tingle. It's been the same ever since, through the good years and the lean years . . . because never have Manchester United sought anything other than the best.

I'm not belittling other clubs when I say this, and in fact I had a great deal of admiration for Liverpool and Tottenham Hotspur; maybe, also, had one of these clubs come in for me, I would have been tempted to sign professional for them. But if it had been between Manchester United and anyone else, there would still have been only one decision for me. Manchester United – every time.

In my time at Old Trafford, United have travelled the world and won supporters in the process. The United States, the Middle East, Australia, the length and breadth of Europe . . . you will find fans of Manchester United everywhere. I've met a fair number of them in my travels, and they are United-daft.

One of these fans from abroad – he lives in Belgium, as a matter of fact – explained why he supported United so avidly this way: 'We come to watch a team where football is played in the right way, attacking all the time.'

That fan has travelled several times just to see United play at Old Trafford, and when he makes a trip, it starts on a Friday and doesn't end until he's back home on a Sunday morning – without having slept. 'Some people say we are crazy to make so long a trip to see United playing, but to see a British football match you do something very special. I'm not alone in coming from the Continent to see an English match.'

United's home-based fans are not alone, either, when they travel from Manchester to see their team play in London, Yorkshire, the Midlands or East Anglia. Wherever they go, fans from other parts of the country also converge, and they all support Manchester United. I've been on grounds one hundred miles from Old Trafford and heard the roar of welcome from our supporters – so much so that it's been little different from playing in a home game.

More than a few United players of the past have served on the backroom side at Old Trafford, and many more have returned to watch their red-shirted successors in action. Once you have been a part of Manchester United, it's almost impossible to let go completely, and I don't deny that I would be sick if I had to leave United.

I have been brought up at Old Trafford, so far as my career is concerned, and it would hurt me tremendously if I were told that the club no longer required my services. Sure, I would go, because when you're not wanted or needed any more, there is no point in staying to fight a losing battle; but even if I left, I would always remember the great times I had had at a truly great club.

In my experience, it's always been a friendly club, and the staff have been a part of that friendly atmosphere. Many of them are people who were working for United when I first joined the club. Time and again, I have seen and experienced the way in which the club makes a point of helping people, when help is needed or sought, and that is something which you don't easily forget. So it would be a major step to have to start again with another club. And my sincere hope is that I never have to face that decision. When I finally do hang up my boots, I want it to be when I have come to the end of my career . . . with Manchester United.

7   Chasing The Title

So far as I'm concerned, my First Division career really began in season 1975–76, because for the first time I was regarded as a regular, and at the end of that term I had played in 41 League matches and scored 10 goals, plus three in Cup competitions. Yet it was a season destined to finish on a note of disappointment in two ways . . . and the close season brought the drama of Tommy Docherty's dismissal as manager.

Manchester United served notice of their intentions by going to Molineux on the opening day of the season and scoring a 2–0 victory over Wolves. At the same time, Queen's Park Rangers were beating Liverpool by a similar margin at Loftus Road and Derby County were drawing 1–1 against Sheffield United at Bramall Lane. No-one then realised that United, Rangers, Liverpool and Derby would become locked in a tremendous tussle for the First Division championship, or that United and Derby would tangle also in the semi-finals of the F.A. Cup, with United going on to Wembley.

More than 55,000 people flocked to Old Trafford for the game against Sheffield United, and we scored a resounding, 5–1 triumph, with Stuart Pearson getting the first two goals (sandwiched by an own goal from Len Badger) and Lou Macari and myself making it a nap hand. After three games, we had maximum points, with Rangers third, behind Newcastle. Believe it or not, but at that early stage Liverpool were down in 13th position while Derby County stood only six places from the bottom of the table.

Liverpool and Derby stuttered on for a bit, while we maintained our winning ways, but after half a dozen matches the Anfield Reds were making their presence felt, as they closed up to fifth place. Derby, too, had climbed to a mid-table position, but at that stage no-one was talking about the League title.

It was mid-October when we began to make people take us seriously as League-championship hopefuls, for we were still competing with Rangers for the top spot, and by then Liverpool and Derby were among the first five. Our biggest test to date came when we travelled to Elland Road to take on Leeds – themselves in sixth position, and rated a reasonable tip for the title.

We pushed the ball about with such assurance that the old stagers of Leeds began to get rattled, and Norman Hunter collected a booking for an offence against Stuart Pearson. We wobbled a bit, defensively, just before half-time, when Leeds missed two excellent chances of scoring, but when the whistle blew we were going in a goal ahead. That was one of the two I scored in the game, and we ran out 2–1 winners. I picked up the ball from a clearance, and hammered a shot home, for my first goal, and the second came when I caught the 'keeper in two minds as I hit a drive from all of 30 yards. I'd kicked off the season with three goals in as many games, and the brace at Leeds did me no harm, either.

Seventeen points from our first dozen matches gave a pointer to our potential, although seven of our games had been played at Old Trafford. We dropped our first home point in a 1–1 draw against Coventry City, and maybe the 52,000 fans who had rolled up expecting a convincing United win went away feeling a bit disappointed; but we didn't make many slips during the first half of the season, and we arrived at the turn of the year still bang in contention for the title.

Our 21st match was a repeat of our first home game, in that the opposition was again Sheffield United, but this time the venue was Bramall Lane, and the scoreline wasn't quite so convincing. On the first occasion we had won 5–1 . . . this time out, we settled for a 4–1 scoreline. Two Pearson goals, another by Gordon Hill and the fourth by Lou Macari, and Manchester United were still up with the League leaders.

At the top were Queen's Park Rangers, then came Liverpool, United and Derby . . . with each club having played 21 matches and each club having collected 28 points. It had been an exhilarating 'first half', with some memorable matches – a 3–2 home win over Spurs, a 2–2 draw in the Maine Road derby game against Manchester City (all four goals came in the space of 12 minutes of the first half), the 2–1 win at Leeds, a 3–1 victory over Arsenal.

There had also been one or two defeats – 1–0 away against Queen's Park Rangers, 3–1 against Liverpool at Anfield, and another 3–1 scoreline when we met Arsenal in the return match at Highbury. That was our third visit to London and the third time we had lost there, so we had begun to feel that there was a jinx on us in the capital.

Arsenal at Highbury had scored the quickest League goal of the season, when they hit United's net after just 12 seconds. And the man in the firing line was Paddy Roche, who had taken over from Alex Stepney in goal.

When Arsenal kicked off, the ball went to Sammy Nelson, who swung it immediately into our goalmouth. Ironically, it was Brian Kidd, by then wearing Arsenal's colours, who nodded the ball into the path of Alan Ball, and he tucked the chance away. I was carried off after the game had been going for less than quarter of an hour – I'd fallen heavily as I tried a shot – and within minutes of David McCreery going on as substitute, the Gunners were firing the ball past Paddy Roche again.

The 'keeper failed to cut out a free-kick from Nelson, and Armstrong knocked the ball towards goal. It seemed there was little danger, with Brian Greenhoff arriving in time to clear – but he hit the ball into the roof of the net. And the chapter of accidents was completed in the final move of the game when Paddy Roche, attempting to deal with an in-swinging corner from Geordie Armstrong, succeeded only in punching the ball into his own net. Our only counter was a goal from Stuart Pearson.

The introduction of Paddy Roche into United's team had been a controversial move by The Doc towards the end of the year, when he announced that in his view, Paddy was the man for the future. Alex Stepney made it clear he didn't agree with Tommy Docherty's assumption, and eventually United's manager had to back-pedal, for Alex regained his place and Paddy dropped back to the obscurity of the reserves.

While he was in the first team, Paddy took a considerable amount of stick from the critics, and even today some people won't let him forget his nightmare experience. I would be the last to rub salt into the wound, and I think I speak for every one of Paddy's team-mates when I say that it was sad to see his confidence crumbling as the goals went in and the pressure on him increased.

Nobody knows better than myself what a struggle it can be to believe in yourself after things have started to go wrong, and no-one envied Paddy his experience. I think he would be the first to agree, however, that the goals which went in during that spell proved crucial in the final analysis – and I'm not laying the blame at Paddy's door, for a goalkeeper is supposed to have a defence protecting him.

I've got to say that I have always felt that if we hadn't conceded the goals during this patchy spell, we would probably have wound up by taking the championship of the First Division. And I'm looking back neither in sorrow nor in anger when I say that. Irrespective of which players were at fault (and I've stressed that there were defensive lapses), the fact remains that goals went against us – and they counted when the crunch came.

The start of 1976 proved a time of success for us, though. In the third round of the F.A. Cup we met and beat Oxford United 2–1 at Old Trafford, and a week later turned the tables on Queen's Park Rangers as we scored a 2–1 home win – with me hitting the second goal. Fifty-eight thousand fans gave us a standing ovation as we left the field, for we had wiped out a goal from Don Givens – a former United player – who had given Rangers a 10th minute lead, and my goal was the clincher. A long-range drive from Brian Greenhoff hit John Hollins, and it bounced right into my path. All I had to do was drive the ball past Phil Parkes.

And that win saw us at the top of the First Division, with 35 points from 25 games. Leeds, with a match in hand, were a point behind, as were Liverpool, with Derby on 32 points. And we earned this tribute from Dave Sexton, the man who is now United's manager: 'United are the best team we've played. They must be in with a good chance of winning the title.' Dave then was the team boss of Rangers . . . and they hadn't given up the battle.

Later, he was to say that with all the title contenders carrying on winning, he felt that something had to give – but he couldn't see what!

In that match against Rangers, we played some beautiful football, and but for Phil Parkes we might have had at least two more goals, for in the second half he produced brilliant saves to foil Lou Macari and Alex Forsyth.

It was interesting to see what other people thought about the championship contest. Gerry Francis, for instance, agreed with his manager – in fact, he went further and said he felt sure we would win something that season. Tony Waddington, then the manager at Stoke, had seen Leeds beat his side, and he was tipping the race to be between Leeds, Liverpool and Manchester United.

Duncan McKenzie, who was playing for Leeds then, looked ahead to the following month when they were due to come up against Liverpool and Manchester United, and said: 'If we can get through those games unbeaten, I think we could go through the rest of the season unbeaten.'

But Lou Macari was one tipster who backed Manchester United. 'The title is there for the taking,' he said, 'and I can see us taking it, if we play like we did today.' Lou wasn't quite right, but he wasn't far off the mark – and the guy who said that United's win over Rangers had ended their title hopes was way out . . . Rangers, as I recollect, went on to pick up around 27 points out of 30, and went closest to pipping Liverpool for the title prize.

The games kept going by, and the title chasers all kept on winning, while in the F.A. Cup Manchester United and Derby stayed on course for Wembley. While Leeds were losing 1–0 at home to Crystal Palace, Derby were knocking out Liverpool with a Roger Davies goal at the Baseball Ground, and United were riding their luck by beating Peterborough 3–1 at Old Trafford. That was two home ties in succession, and each time against a team from a lower division. Queen's Park Rangers, meanwhile, who had drawn at home against Newcastle in the third round, lost the replay; so they could concentrate on the League.

Leeds' exit from the Cup was followed by a 3–0 home

defeat from Norwich, but we beat Birmingham, Liverpool won 4–0 at West Ham and Derby scored a 2–0 win over Coventry. When Leeds did go to Anfield, they lost 2–0, and a 2–0 home defeat by Middlesbrough pushed them further down the table. By then, it was becoming a three-horse race, with Liverpool leading the way.

Along came the fifth round of the Cup, and while Derby had a fairly easy tie against Southend (who were down-table in the Third Division) at the Baseball Ground, we had to travel to Filbert Street for a battle with Leicester. It all went right for us, as Lou Macari and Gerry Daly scored, and though Bob Lee pulled one back, we never really looked like losing our grip on the tie. As for Derby, they had to thank Bruce Rioch for a goal which won their game with Southend.

So side by side with the League battle was the quest for the F.A. Cup, and both Manchester United and Derby County were beginning to see double. At the top of the First Division it was Liverpool (39 points), United (39), Rangers (38) and Derby (36), with Rangers having played 30 matches and the three other contenders 28 games each. And when the sixth-round draw for the F.A. Cup was made, United and Derby were still kept apart . . . we were paired with Wolves, Derby had to take on Newcastle.

A week before the sixth round, Liverpool went to Derby and pinched a point three minutes from the end of the match; it was to prove the start of Derby's slide from the race for the title. Meanwhile, Rangers drew 0–0 at Bramall Lane, and we hammered West Ham 4–0 at Old Trafford. However, it was a different story a week later on the same ground, for John Richards gave Wolves the lead after 58 minutes, and we spent 10 frantic minutes chasing an equaliser before Gerry Daly obliged. So it was a replay at Molineux . . . while Derby had beaten off Newcastle's challenge with a 4–2 victory.

The draw for the semi-finals was made before our replay, and finally Manchester United and Derby were paired together – always provided, of course, that we disposed of Wolves at the second attempt. It didn't look as if we would be in the hunt when Wolves slipped quickly into gear and struck two goals in 21 minutes. The men who did the damage were Richards again, and Steve Kindon.

United took a gamble – for with Lou Macari nursing a foot injury, we pulled him out of the midfield battle and sent on defender Jimmy Nicholl. That meant Brian Greenhoff switching positions. Lou had been a doubtful starter, and even before he kicked off his foot had been 'frozen', so he wasn't arguing when Tommy Docherty made the bold decision to make the switch. He admitted himself that after only a couple of minutes he realised he wasn't really fit for the fray.

The two Wolves' goals had come in as many minutes and though Stuart Pearson pulled one back for us before half-time, the odds were still on the home side. Brian Greenhoff became a hero when he forced extra time with a goal . . . and I ended up being mobbed by my team-mates when I headed what turned out to be the winner. It was a breath-taking tie for the fans to watch.

After our victory over Wolves, I said it would be a tragedy for the game if Manchester United didn't win something that season. I still feel we deserved to do better than finish as runners-up at Wembley and third in the First Division – and that's not detracting from the F.A. Cup-final performance by Southampton, or from the results that Liverpool and Queen's Park Rangers achieved, to head us in the League.

Quite simply, we had confounded all the critics and proved that the bubble hadn't burst. More than that, we had played swashbuckling football right the way through the season, pulled in the crowds at home and on tour and given real value for money when it came to entertainment, as well as results, in practically every game. When you turn on the style like that, you are entitled to feel you deserve some reward.

Another reason for wanting to finish up with a trophy was that if we didn't, people would still claim that Manchester United were far from being a great side, and that they had had luck perched on their shoulders. With Wembley in sight, and six League matches to play, we knew that if we could reel off eight straight wins, nobody could prevent us from doing the double. Two victories, and the F.A. Cup would be ours; six wins, and the League championship would be wrapped up.

Liverpool were coming in for a bit of criticism because of their style of play – they were giving nothing away, and accused of defensive tactics on opponents' grounds. I wasn't one of those who argued against them, because I don't care who it is, if you feel you have sorted out the right formula for your team, then it's right to stick to it, and hang what others say. But that wasn't the Manchester United approach – we were committed to going out every time with the idea of winning . . . and entertaining.

People used to say that we played as if we didn't even consider the possibility of defeat, and to be frank, The Doc had more or less indoctrinated us with this philosophy. There were folk who claimed that Manchester United were a team of runners, but we didn't subscribe to that view. And we set out to prove it when we met Derby County in the semi-final at Hillsborough.

I'm not denigrating Derby when I say they were never really in the hunt – though I'm prepared to accept that, on the day, they didn't play as well as they had done in past performances. That day, they just couldn't seem able to raise their game, and we started off in a higher gear than them. Two goals from Gordon Hill – and they were two of his specials – put the skids under Derby and Manchester United on the road to Wembley, and we played as if the result was never in doubt – even before we had scored, we were looking winners.

We cruised over the semi-final hurdle, and we were still aiming for the double. We had beaten Leeds 3–2 in the return game at Old Trafford, won 4–3 at Newcastle and hammered Middlesbrough 3–0 on our own ground. But we started to stumble a bit in the League when we went to Portman Road and lost 3–0 against Ipswich, sandwiched a 2–1 home win over Everton, then lost 2–1 at Leicester and won 1–0 at Burnley.

By then, Liverpool had only one game to play, and they were on the 58-point mark, while Rangers, on 57 points, also had one match left. Manchester United, in third place, mustered 54 points, but it was still in our hands, for we had three games left, though goal average could come into it.

On the final run-in, Liverpool didn't make any mistakes, for they won their last match and wound up with a total of 60 points – and that was a tremendous blow to Rangers, who had already completed their programme and totalled 59 points. Indeed, Liverpool's title triumph was sealed on a May night at Molineux, where we had scored our dramatic F.A. Cup victory to reach the semi-finals, and when Liverpool chalked up a 3–1 win, it sentenced Wolves to a spell in the Second Division.

I recall the night the title went to Anfield, for the match was broadcast on the radio, and when Steve Kindon shot Wolves into an early lead, it made good news for Rangers skipper Frank McLintock and his team-mates, who were receiving a progress report on the match. By then, we knew that Manchester United's hopes of a double success had evaporated, for our results had seen us falter at the final hurdle and we were striving really for a qualifying place in Europe, as an insurance against defeat at Wembley in the Cup final. But it was still an achievement for us to come a good third, with a total of 56 points, in our first season back in Division 1.

As for the F.A. Cup final, it turned out to be an occasion of drama, joy for Second Division Southampton, and sorrow for Manchester United. Although it was to be merely the first of three Wembley finals in which I was to play during four years as the 1970's came towards a close.

8 Wembley – Behind The Scenes

Now that I've played in three F.A. Cup finals, I can claim to be something of an authority on the subject – and you have my word for it that familiarity definitely does NOT breed contempt. Far from it . . . because I have discovered that while Wembley has become a place I know inside-out, the waiting during the hours which lead up to kick-off time does not become any easier.

One thing I know now, as well: while you tend to look for omens (and some players are extremely superstitious), it's really all down to what happens on the day. We stayed in one hotel before we played Southampton in the 1976 final, and lost; we switched hotels for the 1977 final against Liverpool, and won; we decided that was our lucky hotel, and stayed there before we played Arsenal in the 1979 final . . . and we lost.

Now, perhaps, is a good time to take you behind the scenes during the hours that lead up to the big event. And no matter how many times I go back to Wembley for an F.A. Cup final, I'll never become blasé about it. The stadium may not be the biggest or the most impressive in which I have played, but it certainly generates an atmosphere all of its own on Cup-final day.

As is the case with every other club when the team is away from home, United's players double up, with two men sharing a room in the hotel. My room-mate on tour with United is my Northern Ireland colleague, Jimmy Nicholl, and while we're both quiet characters, we differ in one respect. I'm always a fairly early riser, and even though on tour you get the chance of a lie-in, I find that by around 8.30 I'm ready for up and going down to breakfast.

Jimmy says he'll join me – it's the same promise every time United are playing away – but as I'm leaving the room I look back and see my team-mate sprawled out and still fast asleep in bed. So the result is that he never catches up on breakfast. Normally, I'll find four or five United players down for breakfast – like me, Steve Coppell, Lou Macari, Ashley Grimes and Arthur Albiston enjoy their morning bacon and eggs – and generally I finish by polishing off my sixth cup of tea. I'm a great one for a cuppa – to me, it tastes better than a magnum of champagne – and I drink countless cups of tea during the time we're living in a hotel.

By the time we're finishing breakfast, the remainder of the United players are appearing, and it's around 9.30. They settle for tea or coffee, and some toast. At that stage, with Wembley still more than 24 hours away, nobody is talking about the Cup final and our chances of landing the trophy. By 10 o'clock we're ready for a training session in the grounds of the hotel, and after some exercises to loosen the muscles, we have a light-hearted five-a-side game.

Lunch is on the light side, and I suspect that's because manager Dave Sexton wants to make sure nobody falls asleep during the team talk he gives us in a private lounge later in the afternoon! By then, we're supposed to have done our napping.

And mention of United's manager reminds me that he usually develops a pain in the neck just before a big game is coming up – and, in the case of a Cup final, he follows a pre-match routine designed not to tempt fate! When United went to Wembley in 1979, it was the manager's third trip here, for twice he had led Chelsea to finals, and a couple of days before we played Arsenal he went missing.

He was sticking to the routine he had begun when he was with Chelsea . . . making a trip to visit his mother in Brighton also the excuse to have a hair trim by the barber who had cut it on the eve of previous big occasions. And on the day of the final he wore a grey suit which he first 'christened' when he walked out at Wembley ahead of the Chelsea team as they took on Leeds in the 1970 final.

As for that pain in the neck, for Dave Sexton it's one sure

reminder of the tension that a big game brings for a manager, as well as for the players. Usually, as the great day approaches, he'll awaken in the morning and find that his neck has stiffened up, so that it's difficult for him to turn his head. The muscles become knotted, as the tension begins to get through to him.

On the eve of the Cup final, the manager does his best during the team talk not only to make us well aware of the strong points and weak points of the opposition, but to convince us that we have the ability to prove the better team, on the day. We know all about the skill of Liam Brady, for instance, the danger that Alan Sunderland can spell when he breaks through for goal, the power of Brian Talbot and his readiness to have a shot from long range, and the aerial ability of defenders David O'Leary and Willie Young.

Quite rightly, though, the manager points out that in Joe Jordan we have a striker whose ability to win aerial duels can give us an edge — if we make the best possible use of the flicks from his head. And we all know that it's going to be a tremendous contest between Joe and his fellow-Scot, Willie Young.

The Jordan-Young battle isn't the only thing that's taken into account, and by the time the team briefing has ended each player has a good idea of the kind of job he'll be required to do the following afternoon. Yet you still know, deep down, that one split-second decision — or a moment of indecision — can swing the game for you or against you. And all you can do is be determined to give of your best, right through the 90 minutes — and hope that you hit form.

One event always takes place on the eve of a Cup final. Ted Croker, the secretary of the Football Association, visits the headquarters of each team and explains the pre-match ceremony. He goes through the routine from the moment we walk out of the tunnel, makes sure we know just where to line up, and explains also the way the introductions are made as the VIP's meet the players and officials.

Once this business has been concluded, the players are left with their own thoughts about what might happen the following afternoon, and while you try not to think too much about what lies ahead, it's inevitable that at times you dream of scoring the winning goal, while at other moments you hope you don't make a mistake which brings one for the opposition. But mainly, your fervent desire is to finish up knowing that, whatever the result, you can hold your head high in the knowledge that you haven't let yourself, your team-mates or your club's supporters down. In the words of the Bruce Forsyth catchphrase, you want people to say: 'Didn't he do well?'

Not surprisingly, the team talk and the visit from Ted Croker have ensured that the Cup final is uppermost in your mind, but you try to relax by making the routine as normal as possible. I enjoy a game of snooker, for example, and I reckon I'm fairly good at this game – but I know that to win the title of 'champ' among the United players, I'll have to turn on the style. Jimmy Greenhoff, for instance, is pretty hot stuff at snooker himself.

The hotel has just about every facility possible, and table-tennis is another recreation. When David McCreery was at United, he was the man everybody had to beat. On the other hand, Jimmy Nicholl prefers to spend much of his leisure time solving the crosswords, and he always has a good supply of puzzles on tour.

The evening meal is around seven o'clock, and while you can take your pick of the menu, everyone eats simply – the last thing you want is to wake up during the night with a tummy upset because you've overeaten or had something too rich. IF you can sleep, that is . . . and to make sure that there are no problems on this score, each player is asked if he would like to take a sleeping pill that night.

Few players take up this offer, and I'm not one of them, for usually I get to sleep the moment my head hits the pillow. The one exception was after we had played Liverpool in the 1979 semi-final at Maine Road, and we finished up knowing that a replay lay ahead. We had played so well and deserved to win at the first time of asking, and like my team-mates, I knew we hadn't hit Liverpool with the killer punch.

They had come back from the verge of defeat to snatch a second chance, and that Saturday night I was haunted by the fear that we would be made to pay for it in the replay at Goodison Park.

I relived virtually every kick of the match at Maine Road, figuring out why we hadn't won, and the fact that so many people told us how well United had played didn't ease my worries about the second confrontation. For three nights I slept badly, and it wasn't until we settled into our hotel on the Tuesday, 24 hours before the replay, that I became philosophical about what the next night would bring.

As it turned out, it brought a breakaway goal which was stabbed home by Jimmy Greenhoff, and earned us our place at Wembley . . . and that night I found I couldn't sleep again, because this time the adrenalin was still flowing, as I lived the replay over and over again. But at least I had the satisfaction of knowing we were at Wembley.

The night before the final, there is an 11 p.m. curfew for the players, and I reckon everyone is glad when it's time to troop off to bed. I know that one player who won't lose any sleep is Lou Macari, for the little Scot invariably takes advantage of that sleeping-pill offer before a big game, and it seems to do the trick for him.

It's sleep-in time on Saturday morning – if, that is, you are sufficiently relaxed to achieve such an objective. For the moment you awake, the Cup final is on your mind. You know that in a few hours' time, it will all be happening, and 100,000 people will be shouting and cheering for all they're worth. Half of them for the opposition!

Cup final or not, I'm down for breakfast by 8.30, and so are a few of the regulars. The only rule that morning is that you must be dressed and down for the mid-day meal, so the odds are that you won't see some of the other players until then. But I know that even though they may still be in bed, the chances are that, like me, they're wide awake and maybe watching the television build-up to the match.

Somehow, the hours pass, and it's time for lunch. That's one meal I skip, because I've already had bacon and eggs, and I don't want to overdo it. Brian Greenhoff may be at Leeds now, but I know that his pre-match lunch will still consist of toast; one or two players plump for a big dish of cornflakes; and others settle for a steak or scrambled egg. Nobody risks eating anything that might make him feel slug-

gish—we all know that we've got to be on our toes for up to
120 minutes later on, since extra time is always on the cards
in a Cup final.

I leave my team-mates to finish their lunch and make my
way up to my room, to do a spot of quiet thinking about
what lies ahead. The adrenalin isn't yet flowing . . . but the
nerves are certainly in evidence. It's a bit like sitting in the
waiting room at the dentist's and wondering if the check-up
is going to end with him telling you he'll have to take out
all your teeth. So when Jimmy Nicholl appears and tells me
we're ready for off, it's a relief.

As you step aboard the team coach and look at the faces
of the players, you know they're all feeling the same. It's an
hour's drive to Wembley, and you'll have to run the
gauntlet of the fans – your own shouting their good wishes,
and those of the opposition who aren't exactly strewing your
path with roses! And as you look at those fans, you wonder
which of them will still be smiling, come five o'clock—and
whether YOU'LL be laughing your head off, or wanting to cry.

During the ride to the stadium, the inevitable card schools
are in progress, with players like Lou Macari, Jimmy Nicholl,
Gordon McQueen and Paddy Roche hoping their luck is in.
One or two players prefer to sit quietly reading – Steve
Coppell and Martin Buchan are the bookworms at United
– and others just talk or sit looking through the coach
windows, trying to hide the nerves and give the impression
that it's just another game.

Tommy Cavanagh has one special superstition, and he
has insisted that a Max Bygraves cassette is played on the
coach stereo. There's a concerted chant of abuse from the
players, but it makes no difference. That tape is very much
in evidence before a game, and Cav seems to think it inspires
Manchester United to win. So we have to put up with it.

At last, we have reached Wembley, and we are inside the
dressing-room. By then, the atmosphere and the tension have
really got through to us, and the players are keyed up. We
know, too, that just a few yards away the opposition is in
the same frame of mind. Suddenly, you want to get out on
the pitch and get the thing under way. But the match isn't

due to start for quite a while, so the next-best thing is to walk out and have a look at the ground.

As you make the inspection, you cannot help but look around the stadium, which is filling up with supporters of both clubs, and you try to concentrate on the turf again. But while your mind is still in a bit of a muddle, you can sense that the adrenalin is at last beginning to flow. The nerves are still there, but so is that feeling of anticipation and excitement.

Back to the dressing-room, and there's still an hour to kick-off time. Two of the first players to get stripped and changed into their playing kit are Joe Jordan and Gordon McQueen. Once they're ready, they start up a routine designed to loosen the muscles, and if you're not careful you're liable to get a clip on the ear as one or the other swings his arms about.

Most of the United players have been to Wembley before, either for a Cup final or with their respective international teams. But you get the odd one who is experiencing such an occasion for the first time, and those among you who know what it's all about keep an eye on the newcomer. You're watching for signs of nerves, and you're ready to try to relax the tension for him.   Mickey Thomas, United's latest recruit, was such a player before the 1979 final. Only a year previously, Mickey had been playing in another Cup final – the Welsh Cup – and when Wrexham went to Bangor for the first leg of the final, the game was staged on a small ground in front of just a few thousand fans. Only a few hours earlier, he had sat and watched the F. A. Cup final on television – and, as he said, the two games were worlds apart.

For Mickey, everything had happened at whirlwind pace in just a few months. He had gone straight from school to Wrexham and, while he had become a Welsh international, he had spent much of his time dreaming about playing for a glamour club and savouring something like an F. A. Cup final, with 100,000 people watching. And yet, twice during his career he had come close to turning his back on professional football.

The first time was when, at the age of 18, he just disappeared for a week. Then he returned to the club, and that was that. The second time, after Wrexham had played a match against Walsall, Mickey decided he had had his fill of football, and he left the ground determined that this was the end. He didn't even go home—he took off for Colwyn Bay, where he went to a friend's house.

The official version was that Mickey was ill, but he simply stayed in hiding, and he had made up his mind that he was going to get himself a job in a factory. Eventually, John Neal – who was Wrexham's manager at the time – tracked him down and knocked on the door. Player and team boss had a lengthy heart-to-heart talk, and Mickey was persuaded to return to Wrexham.

The day came when Manchester United forked out £330,000 and Mickey became a player at Old Trafford. As he admitted at the time, it frightened him to death as he looked around and saw all the big-name players. I know that feeling all too well myself . . .

I also knew just how much that first visit to Wembley would be likely to affect Mickey Thomas, who was a naturally nervous person before a game, in any event. And for him, this was the biggest occasion of his life. So the old Wembley hands such as myself kept a quiet eye on our team-mate.

Not only nervous, but superstitious . . . that's Mickey, for once he's in the dressing-room he makes sure that before the match he sits in four different parts of the room. He'll spend a few minutes sitting in one spot, then nip over to another corner of the dressing-room, and move on again until he has completed the sequence.

That Cup-final morning, Mickey had been up earlier than anyone – he was out and about an hour before I put in an appearance, so he'd been on the go already since 7.30 a.m. That in itself showed how the occasion had got through to him, because usually he's one of those players who have a long lie-in. He had played table-tennis, tried his hand at snooker, and been out three times for a walk – by my reckoning, he must have used up enough energy to have taken him through a Cup final before he even reached Wembley.

And he confessed as he walked out for the final, his legs were shaking—though he emerged as one of United's heroes as the game wore on. Not surprisingly, when the end of the match came, Mickey Thomas felt shattered.

The man who does the 'winding up' before a game is Tommy Cavanagh, and words spill from him at a rate of knots. Cav always has to be talking, and immediately before we go out he's trying to key us up to such a pitch that we cannot wait for the action to begin. Maybe, even, we're all glad of the chance to escape from that torrent of words! And Wembley is no different.

The man to have the last word before we go out and face the music is the manager, and Dave Sexton's quietness is in complete contrast with the verbal exhortations of Tommy Cavanagh. Dave goes round to each player and has a quiet, but encouraging word, then he has a collective message for us. Five words which we have come to expect . . . 'Come on, my bonny boys!'

We shake each other's hands, wish team-mates the best of luck, then we're on our way, and as we step outside the dressing-room and reach the tunnel, it seems like a long, cool cavern. Suddenly, you're side by side with the players who are going to do battle with you every inch of the way, and it makes no difference that men such as Pat Jennings, Sammy Nelson and Pat Rice are not only nice guys but team-mates of yours on the international field.

You pass the time of day with them, but you and they know that in a few minutes' time no quarter will be asked or given. You haven't come all this way and battled so hard to get there only to allow them to play the game they want. There's no animosity – just a mutual acceptance that when the whistle goes, friendship flies out of the window and rivalry begins.

It seems a long, long walk to the half-way line, too, and the crescendo of sound which greets you as you emerge from the tunnel tends to take you by surprise, even though you may have heard it all before. You blink a bit, too, as you find the sunlight hitting you, and you tell yourself that it's going to be a test of stamina, as well as skill, in the heat of the bowl.

The pre-match ceremonial is traditional, and you accept this; though you're not really taking in what the VIP's may be saying to you. There are so few minutes to go, then, to the moment the action begins that all you want to do is get the proceedings over and start the kicking-in. For then you will know the waiting is over.

The dignitaries move away, the players of each club move into different halves of the field, and you're kicking the ball to a team-mate. This is what you've really travelled all this way for, prepared yourself for during the past week – to engage in a game of football with a glittering trophy at stake. And when the referee signals that the players should line up for the kick-off, I give my usual clenched-fist salute to my United team-mates, and we're ready for the fray.

That, then, is what it's like when you go to Wembley to compete in the final of the F. A. Cup. And three visits in four years is quite something – though, again, you can believe me when I say that there's a world of difference between walking up the steps to the royal box to collect a winner's medal, and following the victors up there to claim a consolation prize, knowing you've finished second-best.

9   'We Shall Return!'

The luck of the F. A. Cup semi-final draw in the spring of
1976 paired Derby County and Manchester United, and
Crystal Palace and Southampton. Most people had hoped
that United and Derby would be kept apart, and that this
would produce a Wembley classic between two clubs which
had also been engaged in a battle for the championship of the
First Division. When United defeated Derby in such a
decisive manner, and Southampton got the better of Palace,
some folk thought it was merely a matter of United turning
up at Wembley to claim the Cup.

No question about it; the Saints were very much the under-
dogs, rated by most people as second-best to United even
before a ball had been kicked. Southampton's manager,
Lawrie McMenemy, and his players made brave noises
about having as much chance as the opposition, but I suspect
that few people believed them. By the time the great day
came, we were raging favourites to carry off the Cup.

The trouble was, that for all our belief in our own ability,
we had misgivings about what might happen. According to
the experts, we were so certain to win that, psychologically,
this affected us the wrong way. We went into the game wondering if we would live up to expectations.

United started off brightly enough – in fact, during the
first 15 minutes of the match we could have settled it, for we
missed two good chances of sticking away goals. When Steve
Coppell went on a run down the right flank, he got the
ball across and Southampton 'keeper Ian Turner went for
it. But he failed to catch the ball cleanly, and it seemed that
he was in the grip of Wembley nerves, at that point, as
he just managed to push the ball out a few yards ahead of
him. Stuart Pearson and Lou Macari were on the edge of

the six-yard line, but neither was able to apply the finishing touch. Then Gordon Hill got into the action and he made an opening which, normally, Gerry Daly would have accepted gratefully. But Gerry, only eight yards or so from goal, finished with a feeble shot.

There was another scare for the Saints as Gordon Hill broke through, with no-one to stop him, and he tried to lob the ball over the 'keeper as Turner came out. The ball bounced awkwardly, and Gordon couldn't quite get the right timing with his effort . . . even so, from a couple of yards' range Turner did exceptionally well to get his hands to the ball. And this time it stuck.

From then on, Turner grew in stature, and so did Southampton. Any inferiority complex which might have affected them in the early part of the match was banished, and they started to play as if they believed they could not only hold United, but finish as winners. We weren't pushing the passes around first-time any more, and this slowness to move the ball gave the Saints the chance to catch us out with their offside trap. And from being concerned with defence, the Saints started to come at us and test us more, with David Peach overlapping on the left and Peter Rodrigues, the Saints' skipper, marshalling his men with increasing conviction.

I felt that we were still the better side, that we were faster and had more skill, but I could sense that the Saints were growing in confidence, and Peter Osgood and Mick Channon began to give us a hard time.

Ossie was winning the ball in the air too often for my peace of mind, Channon was threatening trouble with his runs at our defence – on one occasion, he went on a 30-yard dash at speed, and though he never really had the ball under full control, it took some alert anticipation by Alex Stepney to avert damage. Alex didn't mess about – he tore out of goal and risked injury as he smothered Channon's close-range effort.

We might just have gone in a goal ahead at half-time, but fortune favoured the brave – in this case, Southampton – when a powerful effort from Gordon Hill, struck on the half-volley, was charged down. And as we walked off for the interval, we knew that while we had had the better of play, spending more time in Southampton's half than they had done in ours, it was still going to be a heck of a battle to break them down in the remaining 45 minutes.

The Saints began the second half as they had finished the first, by showing that they were ready to try conclusions with us all the way, and Martin Buchan had to make a timely interception when Channon was threatening danger shortly after the restart. Peach was giving Steve Coppell a great deal of attention, and this battle between the two was one of the features of the match, with honours just about even at the end. Even so, Steve slipped the Southampton defender once, wriggled his way past another opponent, and got the ball across to Stuart Pearson, who was unmarked.

It always seems that in such a situation, a player should stick the ball into the net, but from experience I know just how deceptive appearances can be. In this instance, the ball was just that fraction too high for Stuart, and he had to twist and turn to get in a shot . . . which zipped just wide of the target. He couldn't be blamed in any way—in fact, he did well to make contact.

The Saints had their moments, as well, and twice they might have had a goal, if the men on the ball had done better. But Nick Holmes and Peter Rodrigues each shot feebly when in a situation where real damage could have been inflicted, and had either of those efforts found the target, I reckon the game would have been won, because we were still miscuing our final passes, and becoming frustrated as we realised that we were not making things go our way.

Frankly, while the game lacked nothing in effort and determination, and while in many respects it was a ding-dong battle between teams of differing styles, the end-product – goals – was sadly lacking, and this was due as much to poor finishing as anything, for both sides had certainly had their chances to score before the controversial winner finally came.

I still look back in anguish on a header which I thought had done the trick, and for once, it wasn't bad finishing that cost us the lead. Steve Coppell wafted over a corner kick, little Lou Macari back-headed the ball and as it went towards the far post I got in a header . . . but the ball hit the wood-work. It was the closest we had gone to nailing the Saints – and again, if that one had counted, I don't think they would have stayed the pace.

More and more, it began to look like the game would go into extra time, and I think that the players on both sides sensed that if a goal did come inside the 90 minutes, it would turn out to be the winner. Indeed, the Saints had a chance as a direct result of my heading against the woodwork, for the ball was cleared, our opponents broke away, and Channon ended up by firing a powerful drive only a yard wide.

There were 17 minutes to go, when the winner was scored. Bobby Stokes had only just rounded off one attack by hammering the ball over the bar, when he got a second bite at the cherry – and this time he made no mistake.

The ironic touch was that the pass which enabled Stokes to score came from a man who, not long earlier, had been playing for Manchester United . . . Jim McCalliog. And even now, I have to admit that Jim lofted a peach of a pass through. It beat our defenders, and Stokes was racing away, with a clear sight of goal. Whether he was worried about being ruled offside or not – and there were one or two argu-ments about that afterwards – the Southampton forward did the right thing. He kept on going – and the whistle didn't go. And as Alex Stepney moved out of goal, Stokes fired in a shot which nestled in the corner of the net.

The arguments about offside were soon ended, when people watched the television replay of the incident. It was seen that Stokes had been swift to anticipate what would happen, and even quicker off the mark when it did, as he sped past Martin Buchan and found that only Alex Stepney barred the way to goal. The referee and linesman were proved to have been right in allowing play to go on and the goal to stand. And with it, Southampton had won the F.A. Cup.

The last few minutes were merely a formality, as South-ampton played with all the composure of a team which knows the trophy is in its grasp. Once ahead, they never looked like making the kind of mistake which might let us in for an equaliser, and the final whistle was just the official signal that the game had been won and lost.

For United, it was a double disappointment, since our hopes of the championship had already been squashed, even though we had a derby game to play against Manchester City the following week. The game itself had not been spectacular, but it had been a gripping contest, and the receipts of £420,000 were a record for a Cup final. We'd been to Wembley to see the Queen (and Prince Philip), we'd played our hearts out, but we were going home without the coveted Cup. And there were a few United players on the verge of tears as they walked off the pitch.

For Tommy Docherty, the defeat was one more in a list of losing appearances at Wembley, for three times he had been disappointed after having high hopes. Yet he was sporting enough to congratulate Lawrie McMenemy when the final whistle blew, and he was thoughtful enough to offer consolation to the United players as they stood with their heads down. Indeed, he made a special point of cheering up Brian Greenhoff, whose face reflected his feelings. Tears for souvenirs . . .

Once a Cup final has been won, the losers always speak brave words, and the phrase that occurs most often is: 'We'll be back next year – to win!' I've often wondered how many of the folk who said those words really believed in them at the time. I can't honestly say I had any deep feeling of conviction that, 12 months after our defeat by the Saints, we would be treading the Wembley turf again. Indeed, I think that when you've lost, the dominant thought there and then is that you might have passed up the only chance you'll ever have.

But the Doc and others proclaimed their belief that we would return, and that declaration of faith was justified, the way things went. In the meantime, we had to return to Manchester without the Cup and face our City rivals a few nights later. That Wembley week-end, the last thing we felt like was playing in what, normally, was regarded not just as a prestige derby game, but one which had to be won. However, on the night, we gave City a 2–0 beating, played better than we had done at Wembley, and left Old Trafford with the cheers of our supporters ringing in our ears.

Gordon Hill, who had been substituted by David McCreery during the Cup final, scored the first goal against City; and Sammy McIlroy, whose header had hit the bar in the final, killed off City by knocking in United's second goal. How I wished that derby game had been the Cup final!

Well, there's many a true word spoken in jest, and those people at Old Trafford who had predicted a return to Wembley 12 months hence lived to see their bold words come true. For in the spring of 1977 Manchester United were competing in the F.A. Cup final for the second year in succession . . . only this time there was a difference. The opposition was Liverpool, and they were rated the favourites to carry off the trophy.

It wasn't that people had lost faith in Manchester United; but Liverpool had already clinched the championship of the First Division, and apart from having reached Wembley they were in the final of the European Cup. They were going for a fantastic treble which had never before been achieved by an English club, and with the first leg of the treble already accomplished, only two teams stood in their way of a hat-trick. Manchester United at Wembley, and Borussia Moenchengladbach, of West Germany, who were their opponents in the European Cup final in Rome the Wednesday after our little tussle.

I suppose that most people outside Manchester were hoping Liverpool would win everything for which they were aiming, and that was not surprising. As the final drew near, both teams were under the microscope, and the glare of publicity was almost blinding. Comparisons were being made not just between two teams of varying styles, but between individual players – and in one assessment I was paired with Ray Kennedy, the man who made things tick on the left side of midfield for Liverpool. 'Kennedy works hard up front, and does a lot of chasing back. And there's danger in his gifted left foot,' was the verdict.

When it came to Sammy McIlroy, the doubts were made very clear. 'He's inconsistent – quick, skilful, capable of anything on his day – but he can also look ordinary.' Well, everyone is entitled to his opinion . . . but on the day I was the one who had the last laugh.

Twice we had tangled with Liverpool in the League, and they had taken three points out of the four, though only one goal had come between us. In the Old Trafford game in the February, Liverpool had settled for denying us space, with their 4–4–2 formation, and it got them a 0–0 draw, though more than 57,000 spectators were possibly a little bit disappointed that there hadn't been more fireworks. And when we went to Anfield for the return game, in the early days of May, more than 53,000 people had to settle for a single goal.

Liverpool had reached Wembley after two semi-final matches against their great rivals, Everton, and they had been rated lucky to get a second chance, after snatching a 2–2 draw. But they had scored a convincing, 3–0 victory in the replay, and earned the right to meet United. More than one United player had been rooting for Everton to win – as Lou Macari put it, 'I really felt we would be able to beat them at Wembley.' And now that it was Liverpool, little Lou said straight out what many people were feeling . . . the prospect was 'a frightening thought . . . frightening, in that Liverpool have so many men who can score goals. All the way from right-back to outside-left.'

But, again like the rest of us, Lou believed that if we hit top form, we could take the F.A. Cup – and certainly we had every incentive, after having lost to Southampton the previous year. Tommy Docherty introduced a note of humour into the arguments that were raging about the teams when he suggested that with Liverpool being League champions and bidding for the European Cup, they might be prepared to let Manchester United walk off with the F.A. Cup. But we all knew there was no chance of that happening – Liverpool want to win everything for which they compete.

Still, we had beaten stiff opposition in our semi-final, and Liverpool couldn't be that much tougher than Leeds, who had fallen to goals from Jimmy Greenhoff and Steve Coppell, though Allan Clarke had netted from a spot-kick for them.

And our League matches with Liverpool had both been close affairs.

Looking back, I'm still not certain if being the under-dogs put us under less pressure than Liverpool, for while they were going for that treble, we faced the risk of coming out losers for the second year in succession – and that meant we were under pressure, as well. I think, also, that when the teams went out to do battle at Wembley, United's players were more apprehensive than Liverpool's – and in the opening stages it showed, for Liverpool soon seemed to slip into gear, and they threatened to take us apart.

The experts had predicted that we would be penalised by the absence of Stewart Houston at left-back, for he had been injured; and teenager Arthur Albiston was the player whom United pitched into the big game. On the day, Arthur was one of the great successes of the United team, playing with the coolness of a veteran, and when United scored first, it looked as if Arthur would be walking up the steps to the royal box to pick up a winner's medal.

But Liverpool were not disposed to give up so easily, and my heart sank when Jimmy Case seized on the ball, swivelled and fired home a magnificent equaliser. It wasn't often that Liverpool gave anyone a second chance, and we had had ours when we had taken the lead. But the goals hadn't dried up . . . there was still one more to come, and it arrived as United broke away down the right and had the Liverpool defence at full stretch.

Ray Clemence had realised the danger, and he was already making his move to cover the situation, as Lou Macari let fly for goal. It's anybody's guess what might have happened, if the ball had gone straight for the target – but Jimmy Greenhoff, sharp as ever, was there to introduce the element of surprise, as he deflected the ball. And before anyone realised what was happening, it was in the Liverpool net.

True to their reputation, Liverpool never gave up. Indeed, they pressed harder than before, in their efforts to get an equaliser. There was certainly no thought in their minds about the gruelling business of extra time and a European Cup final the following Wednesday. They were simply intent on not losing the F.A. Cup final . . . and the European Cup, meanwhile, could take care of itself.

They almost succeeded in getting that goal, too – Ray Kennedy went so close in the dying minutes that my heart skipped a beat – but the game didn't go to extra time, and when the final whistle sounded, it was Manchester United who had won the Cup and Liverpool who had been denied the treble.

Liverpool's players bravely did a lap of honour and saluted their fans, but you could see that they had their heads down, they were so disappointed. And while I was overjoyed, I had to feel sorry for them. I knew that feeling from just a year earlier.

Liverpool returned to Merseyside straight away, to resume training for their European final, and we had a celebration banquet in London, then returned to a welcome in Manchester which eclipsed anything I had ever seen. It was estimated that three quarters of a million people turned up to salute our arrival with the F.A. Cup.

Little did we realise, as we rounded off our second season back in Division 1 with that Cup-final climax that before the start of a new campaign, Tommy Docherty would have taken his departure of Manchester United, for during the close season the axe fell. So I never saw him again in his role of United's team boss, though I would be less than fair if I didn't add that he certainly left his impression on all the players.

I know manager Dave Sexton would be the first to agree that the team which beat Liverpool at Wembley was The Doc's team. He had turned Old Trafford inside-out during the few seasons he spent there, and so many players had come and gone. It all seemed to happen while Tommy Docherty was the man in charge – relegation, promotion, third in the First Division and two F.A. Cup finals . . . you don't forget such experiences.

United, under The Doc, developed a style of swashbuckling football which became almost a trademark. And the one question which will never be answered is: how long could we have kept up that attitude of all-out attack? – My own view is that Manchester United would maintain their crash-bang style just as long as Tommy Docherty was the boss, because when one player started to flag, he would have had no hesitation in going out and signing someone fresh to replace him. How successful the style would have been is a different matter, for other clubs would have caught on and produced their own counter, over a few seasons.

10   The Final We Threw Away

Matt Busby, Wilf McGuinness, Frank O'Farrell, Tommy Docherty . . . and then it was Dave Sexton who followed as Manchester United's manager. I was even beginning to get used to the idea of working for a new boss every few seasons. And if my experience as a player has taught me one thing, it's that I don't want to become a manager when I hang up my boots, because I think the job carries too much pressure. I'll settle for becoming a coach and passing on my knowledge to the young players.

Obviously Matt Busby had been respected right through his time as United's manager, and it was only the passing years which decided him the time had come to step down from the job. Wilf McGuinness? – He'd been one of the boys himself, and maybe I'm biased somewhat in his favour, because I liked him, and I could sense the problems which arose when he was put in charge of players who had been his equals and, in some cases, won more honours in the game.

Under Wilf United had reached two semi-finals, and other managers didn't even get that far with their clubs, yet they still kept their jobs. Having said that, I must add that such managers were not at Manchester United, and I'm sure you'll know what I mean. At Old Trafford the standards are exceptionally high – and so are the demands.

I think Matt Busby must have been saddened by Wilf's ultimate fate, because of his friendship with Wilf and the length of time he had known him. If it was a big decision to give Wilf the job in the first place, it must have been an even bigger one to pull him out. Frankly, I was sorry to see Wilf go, and I know that leaving Manchester United almost broke his heart.

I cannot say I ever really got to know Frank O'Farrell

closely, though he never did me any harm, and he was responsible for giving me a chance of first-team football when he pitched me into the derby game against Manchester City. I think that decision says something for Frank O'Farrell's courage and willingness to back his own judgement, especially since John Aston had become the recognised stand-in for Denis Law. At the end, Frank's departure was sudden – one minute he was United's manager, the next he seemed simply to disappear, for we never saw him take his leave.

With Tommy Docherty, there had been a love-hate relationship among the players, and half of them were genuinely sorry to see him go, while I reckon the other half had few regrets, though they might have felt that his dismissal was not handled as diplomatically as it might have been. I'm certain that no-one could have been sicker than The Doc himself about being fired, for no-one knew better than he did that Manchester United is one of the few clubs where you have the job of a lifetime. When you move on from Old Trafford, the only way is down – and that's said with no disrespect to other clubs.

Consider that Tommy Docherty had left the job of managing Scotland's international team, and you realise what taking charge at Manchester United must have meant to him. I've heard him describe the United job more than once as the best job in the world and, in his own words, 'if you leave here you go down a step.' That's what he used to say to players.

Dave Sexton himself admitted that the United job was one that managers dreamed about – and I'm sure it must have taken a lot to make him uproot, after all the years he had spent in the London area. Yet he had no hesitation in accepting United's offer, though, being a realist, he recognised that it was also his greatest challenge to date, even though he came to Old Trafford with the reputation of being one of the best coaches in Britain.

Dave and The Doc are as different in temperament as cheese and chalk, but when I heard he was coming to Old Trafford my reaction was that United couldn't have chosen a better man for the job. After having worked under

The managers under whom Sammy McIlroy has served at Manchester United . . . Sir Matt Busby, who signed him; Wilf McGuinness; Frank O'Farrell; Tommy Docherty and Dave Sexton.

The brothers . . . Jimmy and Brian Green-hoff. Jimmy's goal won the F.A. Cup for United in 1977, and his semi-final replay goal in 1979 took United to Wembley, Jimmy finally had a battle of his own to fight . . . against injury and for Brian, the parting of the ways came when he moved to Leeds United.

Wembley, 1977 — and two different views, dependent on whether you played for Liverpool or Manchester United, Liverpool's players are dejected, as they troop off the pitch after their defeat. Below: United's players are jubilant, as they take the F.A. Cup with them into the dressing-room bath.

Manchester United's playing squad in the days of Tommy Docherty . . . and, under the management of his successor, Dave Sexton, they pose with the Charity Shield.

Big-money buys of the 1970s, and a home-grown star. Above: Gordon McQueen and Joe Jordan. Below: Gary Bailey, who arrived at Old Trafford as an unknown and, under the guidance of former United goalkeeping ace Harry Gregg. he has become an England Under-21 player.

The international scene — and it's Emlyn Hughes who comes off second-best for England, as Sammy McIlroy goes for goal.

A player who claims a place in Sammy McIlroy's all-star Manchester United team . . . John Fitzpatrick (extreme right), in action against Liverpool. Sadly Fitzpatrick's career was cut short by injury.

A get-together of internationals, as Northern Ireland's Ronnie Blair takes his testimonial match at Oldham Athletic. He was supported by Steve Heighway (Liverpool and the Republic of Ireland), Sammy McIlroy, Manchester United's assistant manager, Tommy Cavanagh (who was also second in command with the Northern Ireland team), and Allan Hunter (Ipswich Town and Northern Ireland).

You could call this the United Nations. On the front row, England's Steve Coppell, Sammy McIlroy (Northern Ireland) and Mickey Thomas (Wales). From left to right at the back: Tommy Cavanagh (Northern Ireland), Gordon McQueen (Scotland), Paddy Roche (Republic of Ireland) and Dave Sexton (England Under-21 team boss).

Left: It's the F.A. Cup, and United are involved in a replay against Wolves at Molineux in 1976. Here's the goal by Sammy McIlroy which brought United a 3–2 victory in the quarter-final . . . and you can see what Sammy thinks about it.

Below: The massed ranks of the Manchester United supporters, as they greet their team on their return from Wembley in 1977.

Right: Wembley, 1977, and Manchester United have just scored in the F.A. Cup Final against Liverpool. Marksman Stuart Pearson is being mobbed by Steve Coppell, Lou Macari (No. 10), Sammy McIlroy and Jimmy Nicholl.

Below: It's all over, bar the shouting, and Tommy Docherty leads Manchester United's victory parade with the F.A. Cup, after the 1977 final against Liverpool.

Wembley, 1979 . . . and Sammy McIlroy puts Manchester United level against Arsenal when he beats 'keeper Pat Jennings — his Northern Ireland team-mate — to hit United's second goal. No doubt about the reaction of Mickey Thomas and Gordon McQueen as they salute Sammy . . . but United's brave bid for victory was ended by a breakaway winner from the Gunners.

The 1976 F.A. Cup final, in which Manchester United lost against Southampton, whose marksman was Bobby Stokes. Here you see United's Gerry Daly and Saints' Nick Holmes in a duel for possession.

August, 1977, and United, as F.A. Cup winners, take on League-champions Liverpool in the F.A. Charity Shield at Wembley. In the thick of the action is Stuart Pearson, striving to score for United — and at the other end of the pitch, it's skipper Martin Buchan and Jimmy Nicholl doing a spot of tidying-up for United.

him for three years, I haven't had any reason to revise my opinion. He's a man who doesn't have a lot to say, whose style isn't flamboyant; but he's a man who thinks deeply about the game. And he loves football.

I'm certain I speak for the rest of my United team-mates when I say that every player at Old Trafford wants to do well, not just for himself, but for Dave Sexton, because of the manager's attitude towards the game. There was a time during season 1978–79 when United were not playing too well, and the fans began to get restless – indeed, some of them started to become vocally critical of Dave Sexton.

When The Doc had been the boss, his name was hardly ever out of the papers; but it seemed that it was hard work to get even a word out of Dave Sexton for print. I suppose the United fans couldn't believe there was such a difference in style between two men, and they probably felt that this was being reflected in the team's performances. So they began to get on Dave's back.

I felt that in doing so they were being rather unfair, that they were being a bit too quick on the draw, especially when voices were heard calling for him to go. I was glad things turned out for the better.

Dave's arrival, of course, raised the inevitable questions. Would he encourage United to play in the style developed by The Doc? Would he make changes in the team, and would he be wheeling and dealing as The Doc had done in the transfer market? – The answers did not come overnight, but when Dave Sexton made his moves, it became clear that he was just as much his own man as Tommy Docherty had been, and that he didn't lack the courage of his convictions.

The arrival of two players – Joe Jordan and Gordon McQueen – from Leeds United meant that Manchester United had spent going on for £850,000, and there were people who, in the early days, were quick to suggest that the money might have been used better, for neither Joe nor Gordon registered as an immediate hit with the fans. The plain truth of the matter was that they needed time to settle down into the team, because they had come from a totally different set-up at Elland Road.

D

For some reason which I've never been able to fathom out, it seems that the Leeds players hadn't much love for their opposite numbers at Old Trafford – Gordon told us that every time we lost, the Leeds dressing-room would be jumping for joy. Maybe it was because Manchester United had built up a good record on their visits to Leeds during the past few years – and we also beat them in the F.A. Cup semi-final of 1977. So perhaps it's natural that the Leeds lads should take some pleasure from seeing our downfall now and then.

Both Joe and Gordon had to take some criticism as they tried to fit into the Manchester United pattern of play, and they were honest enough to acknowledge that it wasn't something they could achieve overnight. Joe reckons that people are entitled to their opinions, but he's more concerned with the reaction from the fellows he trains and plays alongside week by week. He looks at things from the standpoint of a real professional.

United's manager, too, endured the criticism stoically during the early part of season 1978–79, and was content to let the team do the talking for him. As time went by, and the newcomers began to fit into the picture more and more, the criticism became muted, though there was another outburst when Gordon Hill was sold to Derby County, then managed by The Doc.

The United fans had often acclaimed Gordon for his spectacular goals, and he had become a firm favourite with many people in the crowd, but Dave Sexton felt that while his contribution as a marksman was not to be dimissed, United needed a left-sided player who could knit more effectively into the team pattern. And when Gordon was allowed to leave, it didn't mean nothing was happening in the search for a replacement. The arrival of Mickey Thomas was Dave Sexton's answer, and I don't believe anyone would dispute that Mickey has done an excellent job, though in a different kind of way to Gordon.

As the season progressed, United promised to make a challenge for the championship, then we faded a bit, and it was at the end of 1978 that the criticism became most vocal, as Liverpool played us and cruised to a 3–0 victory at Old

Trafford, then West Brom followed up by whacking us 5–3 on our own ground. Everyone at the club felt, around that time, that it was a testing period.

It was the F.A. Cup that turned the tide, as we started to put it all together, though not without one or two scares. In the third round, we had the good fortune to be drawn at home against Chelsea, a club already struggling to retain First Division status, and goals from Steve Coppell, Ashley Grimes and Jimmy Greenhoff saw us safely over that hurdle. The fourth round was tougher, because we counted ourselves a bit lucky to get away with a 1–1 result against Fulham at Craven Cottage, thanks to a Jimmy Greenhoff deflection.

Jimmy maintained his record of scoring in every round when he got the only goal in the replay against Fulham, and I think we surprised quite a few people when we went to Colchester for what was a tough fifth-round assignment and came away with a victory at the first time of asking. Again, it was thanks to a Jimmy Greenhoff goal.

By then, Jimmy was the darling of the United fans and the team as a whole had shown that it could put up a fighting display – so much so that we were beginning to have distinct visions of a return to Wembley, though no-one was saying so openly. And we were not ready to tempt fate when the sixth round demanded that we should meet Tottenham at White Hart Lane, though we had the confidence that we could get through, even if it meant a replay. Which it did.

The hero of the match at Tottenham, from our point of view was Mickey Thomas, and his equaliser did him a world of good, for it boosted his general confidence and – equally important – swung the fans round to his side. And when we met Spurs in the Old Trafford replay, United had every one of their fans rooting for them. The earlier criticism had been forgotten; the faithful were once more united in backing their team. And that was good news for Joe Jordan, who had come back after injury and proved the manager's gamble to be right as he scored the first goal, while I got the one which clinched victory and a semi-final place.

Joe was on the mark again in the Maine Road semi-final against Liverpool (Brian Greenhoff hit the other in our 2–2 draw), and we knew we had done enough to win. But we made no mistake in the Goodison replay, and again Mickey Thomas proved his worth as he put over the cross for Jimmy Greenhoff to score the winner.

That victory compensated for the defeat we had suffered against Liverpool on our own ground a few months earlier, and memories of our lapses in other matches were banished as we took the high road to Wembley. There were one or two scares along the way, for the Greenhoff brothers became doubtful for the final, and it was touch and go during the last few days of our build-up whether Jimmy, in particular, would make it. But the doubts were ended when Brian was named as substitute and his brother declared himself fit to line up against Arsenal.

There were so many fascinating things about this Wembley duel, even before it was staged. Brian Talbot, for instance, had played in the 1978 final for Ipswich, and finished up on the winning side against Arsenal – who, as Manchester United had been in 1976 (when we lost to Southampton), started out as firm favourites. Now Talbot was poised to become the first player to win F.A. Cup medals with two different clubs in successive seasons . . . and, of course, the Gunners themselves were all out to make up for that defeat they had suffered against Ipswich 12 months previously.

On United's side there were Gordon McQueen and Joe Jordan, who had cost the club more than £800,000 in transfer fees, while their counterparts for the Gunners, David O'Leary and Frank Stapleton, might so easily have rendered the expenditure unnecessary, had matters turned out differently, for David and Frank both had trials at Old Trafford before signing up with the Gunners.

Both players hailed from Dublin, but the first time they had met was when they turned up at The Cliff, United's training ground, after having been invited to spend Easter holidays showing their paces in the trial games. That was in Frank O'Farrell's time as manager at United, and a former United player, Shay Brennan, had specifically recommended O'Leary – indeed he featured in the same trial side as Jimmy Nicholl.

But whereas Jimmy put pen to paper for the Old Trafford club, the two lads from Dublin decided, after a visit to Highbury, that this was where their future in football lay, and so on a May day in 1979 they found themselves ranged in opposition to United, instead of playing for the Old Trafford club.

There were other features about the final – my international team-mates, Pat Jennings, Pat Rice and Sammy Nelson, would be doing their best to make sure that I finished up on the losing side, for once, while Liam Brady was out to make up for the disappointment of the previous year by showing that he could take command of a game and make it go his team's way. And the giant Scottish defender, Willie Young, faced a battle against Joe Jordan which, everyone was convinced, would be a fascinating affair, for neither man was given to pulling back from a challenge.

There was also a query about how our young goalkeeper, Gary Bailey, would react in front of 100,000 fans. He hadn't even played a full season in top-flight football, while at the other end Pat Jennings was a veteran of hundreds of big-game occasions. So it all added up to the promise of a cut-and-thrust duel . . . but I don't think anyone envisaged just how this was going to turn out to be one of the most dramatic finals ever staged at Wembley, as it ended with victory for Arsenal and glory for United in defeat.

If beating Liverpool in 1977 had been the highlight of my career, losing to Arsenal brought the worst moment of my footballing life – worse, even, than when I was out of action for months after the car crash. And I've still to be convinced that we didn't throw the game away, for when we equalised in the dying minutes, Arsenal were rocking and ready for the knock-out blow.

I don't mind admitting that when the whistle finally blew, there were tears in my eyes, and I felt choked; not only with disappointment, but with frustration, for I knew that we had been caught by a sucker punch. Today I can look back on that final coldly and dispassionately, and as I go through the various parts of the game, I still feel that the Cup should have come to Manchester.

Apart from the drama of our late, two-goal rally, I believe that even before we scored, we had put the Gunners under a great deal of pressure, and that despite the two-goal lead they forged, Manchester United hadn't gained the rewards their play had deserved.

I've got almost a photographic memory for incidents during matches, and I can recall plenty of things that happened during that final, just as I can relive moments of the finals we played in 1976 and 1977. For instance, I know that Joe Jordan gave Willie Young a hard time of it in the air, and that we could easily have been a couple of goals ahead before Arsenal had scored.

Only a few months previously, Joe had been fighting to win the United fans over to his side, and his emergence during the later rounds as one of our strong men had not been achieved without a lot of gritty effort and sweat, for he had won a battle for fitness to stake his Wembley claims, and proved manager Dave Sexton had been right to gamble with him in ties which immediately preceded the final.

At Wembley, he had the United fans on his side, and he responded to their cheers in no uncertain manner. Early on, he soared above Willie Young to clip a powerful header just wide of goal, and he won another aerial duel to flash a header over the bar. Had either of those efforts counted, we would have given Arsenal something to worry about; instead, the Gunners scored. But when David Price got past Martin Buchan, he still managed to mishit the cross . . . yet he saw Brian Talbot on the spot to force the ball past Gary Bailey.

That goal was a sickener for us, but we fought back, and shortly afterwards Pat Rice had little alternative but to bring me down when I broke away on the left. That foul earned him a booking, though the trip didn't do me any physical harm. Then Joe Jordan was at it again, selling a dummy as he let a cross from Jimmy Nicholl go by him, and as Mickey Thomas switched the ball to Jimmy Greenhoff, the United man turned and hammered a first-timer only inches over the bar.

With half-time looming, we were still well in the game,

then – just a couple of minutes from the interval – Arsenal struck what, at the time, seemed to be the killer blow. For once, we allowed Liam Brady some space inside our penalty area, and he crossed a perfect ball for Frank Stapleton to knock home. My heart sank – and a minute later, I was unhappier still, as I tangled, not for the first time, with Brian Talbot. Four times he'd caught me with late tackles from behind, and I was sporting a swollen lip, as well, but the interval gave me a chance to cool down, as we sat in the dressing-room and listened to Dave Sexton and Tommy Cavanagh weighing matters up.

They both had some pointed things to say to us, but the theme of that half-time heart-to-heart was that if we WERE going to wind up as losers, then at least we should let Arsenal know they'd been in a battle. It was up to us to contest the game every inch of the way. And the restart saw us doing just that.

Arthur Albiston broke down the left and got in a cross which Gordon McQueen – adding weight to our attack – headed just over the bar; then Pat Jennings had to save brilliantly, to deny Lou Macari a goal, and the 'keeper made another fine save as Steve Coppell hit a left-foot volley for goal.

Four minutes from time, and Arsenal were looking surefire winners – and giving the appearance that they thought they had it wrapped up, for they had sent on substitute Steve Walford. But United showed that they were not quite finished, as Steve Coppell sent in a free-kick from the right, Joe Jordan hit the ball into the six-yard box, and Gordon McQueen swept it past Pat Jennings. Two minutes later, and Steve chipped a marvellous pass to send me away. I checked inside Sammy Nelson, nutmegged Walford, and slipped the ball past Jennings as he dived at my feet.

Never in my life have I experienced such a magical moment on a football field – I was certain I'd scored the goal that would take the game into extra time. And I could see that Arsenal's players had their heads down. Manchester United would overpower them in the extra half-hour . . .

But the final devastating blow was still to come, for

Arsenal kicked off, Liam Brady slipped the ball to Graham Rix on the left, and when he crossed, Alan Sunderland was on the spot to stab it home. And it was too late for us to get another goal.

I'll always feel that was the final we threw away, because we were caught on the rebound – and every professional knows that it's when a team has scored a goal it is at its most vulnerable. We were still savouring my equaliser, still up on cloud nine, instead of concentrating on stopping Arsenal for the remaining moments of the match. If we'd done our job properly, we would have made sure the ball went anywhere but to an Arsenal player, and we would have killed them off in extra time.

As I look back on that game, I can see Arthur Albiston sitting on the ground, staring at the ball in United's net after the Gunners had struck their winner. Like me, he was dazed by what had happened, and the picture of despair.

It had all happened in a flash, as the ball came over from Graham Rix on the left and flew over the outstretched arms of 'keeper Gary Bailey. Arthur was coming in, all set to head the ball for a corner, when it seemed to dip sharply and landed at his feet. The worry then was that in trying to whip the ball away, Arthur might put it into his own goal – but before he could even make his move, Sunderland's foot was making contact, and as Arthur went down, the ball was in the net.

So Manchester United went down, as the 1979 F.A. Cup final ended in dramatic fashion, and my goal counted for absolutely nothing. I was shattered, and so were my team-mates, and I can tell you that there is all the difference in the world between attending an after-match banquet where you are parading the Cup, and one where the trophy is missing.

We had a banquet that night, and right through the meal I kept on thinking about the match and going over every move. For Mickey Thomas, it was even worse – he missed most of the evening, because he felt ill. Undoubtedly, it was the reaction after his first Wembley appearance and the shattering effect the finale had on United.

He emerged from the dressing-room an hour after the game feeling numbed and sickly, head and eyes aching, and scarcely with it. In an effort to conquer the sickness he took a few aspirins, but in the end he just had to leave the dinner table and take himself off to bed.

As the evening wore on, I began to feel a bit better about things, and I suppose that finally I could say it hadn't been a bad night, but when I awoke the next morning and read the newspapers, it rammed it home to us again just what it meant to have lost the Cup after such a tremendous comeback.

We knew that we had still to return to Manchester and face the fans there – but this time without the Cup – and that wasn't something to which I was looking forward. But there was no ducking out of it, and in the afternoon we were on the final stage of our journey home.

We left the train and boarded an open-top bus on the outskirts of Manchester . . . and it was incredible how many people had taken the time and trouble to assemble for our arrival. All the way along the route there were fans cheering us and giving us words of encouragement, but it was when we reached the city centre that it really hit us.

The square in front of the town hall was jampacked. Some of those hundreds of thousands of fans had travelled from different parts of the country, and many of them had taken up position in the early hours of the morning, just to make sure they didn't miss our return.

I had thought our homecoming in 1976 was exciting, and our return in 1977 couldn't have been bettered – but it was. And it made me realise what Manchester United mean to so many people. They can even accept us losing, provided we go down fighting, and in style. And if there was one thing above all for which I was grateful, it was the fans' warm-hearted greeting when Dave Sexton said his piece. They showed him that they were with him all the way, and it must have been like music to his ears as they roared their welcome and chanted his name.

'The boss' is usually immaculately dressed and hides his emotions behind a calm exterior, but for once I could see he was shaken out of his stride and deeply affected by the demonstration of loyalty and faith from the massed supporters. It was as if they were saying : 'You're one of us now!' And I was delighted for our manager.

11   Dave Sexton's Style

What would your feelings be, if you were asked to take charge as manager of Manchester United? – Since Sir Matt Busby stepped down, the club has seen Wilf McGuinness, Frank O'Farrell and Tommy Docherty come and go, for various reasons, and Dave Sexton became the fourth incumbent of the managerial chair at Old Trafford on a July day in 1977. Since when, he has had his problems as well as moments which promised success.

Every football fan in the country can manage better than the team boss who's making the decisions at any club – that's probably stating the obvious, because football followers everywhere always reckon they could pick the right team to win a match – and there isn't a side in the country that wins every game.

When Nottingham Forest took Liverpool to a replay in the League Cup final of 1978, the game was staged at Old Trafford, and Forest – who had survived a pounding at Wembley – were penned back in defence for much of the match again, then finished up as winners from a penalty. After the game, Liverpool supporters were bitterly disappointed, and some of them were expressing their views in no uncertain manner.

According to them, team selection had been wrong, some of Liverpool's players just couldn't play, others were over the hill . . . so the criticisms were tossed back and forth. And it was the same after we had knocked Liverpool off the Wembley trail in the F.A. Cup semi-final replay at Goodison Park in 1979. The Liverpudlians were venting their disappointment again.

That was only human, I suppose, and a natural reaction after the supporters had built up their hopes and – let's be been their team have most of the play in the second meeting with United . . . though I suspect that at the end of the first tie, when Liverpool had snatched a 2–2 draw in the dying minutes, their feelings must have been simply of relief that their team was getting a second bite at the cherry.

Liverpool fans, like those of Manchester United, are among the most fanatical in Britain. Correction, in the world. And it's easy to see why both sets of fans become unhappy when things don't go right for their team, because the standard which has been set by each club throughout the past two or three decades has been so high. Which means that expectations are always high.

This, then, was the situation when Dave Sexton arrived at Old Trafford as the successor to Tommy Docherty. And, like it or not, any manager of United will be judged not just on his own achievements, but in comparison with the achievements of Matt Busby when he was in charge. In just the same way, Bob Paisley had to follow a master in Bill Shankly at Liverpool, so the top job at Old Trafford or Anfield cannot fail to be a hot seat.

I mentioned great expectations, and going back to the reign of Wilf McGuinness, let me remind you that he took United to two semi-finals . . . and that was still below the standard required.

Frank O'Farrell had a spell when the team was riding high at the top of the First Division, and the championship looked to be a distinct possibility. But the team slipped from the pinnacle, and the talk was then concerned with relegation. The descent to the Second Division came during Tommy Docherty's time, and possibly people wondered if The Doc would keep his job – but there must be a limit to the turn-over of managers, even at a club where the demand is for constant success.

The Doc stayed, and took United back to the top flight at the first time of asking, then to Wembley in 1976 and 1977. And it's no secret that it wasn't managerial failings which cost him his job. Which brings us back to Dave Sexton.

Apart from the knowledge that continued success was the

goal, United's new manager had another burden on his shoulders, for Tommy Docherty had always been good for quotes, always been a headliner . . . and that just wasn't the new manager's style. In his own quiet way, Dave Sexton can be just as determined as The Doc, just as set on success – but he doesn't go shouting the odds.

He made one pledge when he was appointed United's manager: 'I want to see the team winning and playing attractively. Which comes first? – It must be winning.'

There came a time when Manchester United were neither winning nor playing attractively, though it was for a relatively brief spell, but Dave Sexton then found himself the target for a great deal of criticism from supporters. It all came right, despite defeat by Arsenal in the 1979 F.A. Cup final, because Manchester United produced the kind of performances which the fans had become accustomed to expect.

Ironically, it could so easily have been Dave Sexton who was celebrating victory with Arsenal, instead of consoling the players of Manchester United, because in July, 1977, he had to decide which should be his destination – Highbury or Old Trafford. He turned down the chance to take his coaching talents to Arsenal, and – in his words – took 'about 30 seconds' to accept the offer from United of a three-year contract, though he admitted : 'I've got to be honest and say the image of Manchester United overawed me, to a certain extent.'

He wasn't the first and he won't be the last to harbour such feelings . . . I'll never forget how I felt when I first walked through the doors at Old Trafford.

But he was also realistic enough to appreciate that the job of managing Manchester United was the peak of ambition for anyone in football, because he knew that on past history, the club was always aiming for the top. Which meant the League championship and the European Cup.

Irrespective of the arguments about the dismissal of Tommy Docherty, the fact remained that he had left the club, and I must say that if there had to be a new manager, Dave Sexton was the right man at the right time – though I'm certain he has had to learn a few things on the way, and I am not referring to coaching or tactics.

I'm referring now to the passionate interest people around Manchester take in United and City, to the way people in the north of England generally live for their football and their favourite team. I know there are local rivalries in London, but I don't think they are as intense as those generated in Manchester, on Merseyside or in the North-East. And Lancashire in particular has always been a hot-bed of football fervour.

For the first time in his career – and he was 47 when he accepted the job at United – Dave Sexton left the London surroundings he knew so well. I don't know if he was homesick at first, as I was when I came over from Belfast as a youngster, but I can appreciate the difficulty of uprooting and settling into a strange place after being so familiar with one spot for so long.

Frank Blunstone was United's assistant manager when Dave Sexton took charge, and he had known Dave for 30 years, so he was well qualified to pass an opinion. Two things Frank Blunstone said stand out in my mind. 'Dave can be twice as hard as Tommy Docherty – when he shouts, people jump, because he rarely raises his voice.' I wouldn't say I've seen people literally jump since we got a new boss at Old Trafford, but I do know people take notice when he speaks . . . and so far he hasn't needed to raise his voice above his usual quiet tones.

The other thing Frank said was that United's manager was flexible, open to changes in the game. 'If United's style needs a little modification, he'll modify it. He moves with the times and ahead.' No-one can argue that Dave Sexton hasn't modified the team since he arrived, for we have seen costly players recruited. And, in the process, the style has changed somewhat, as well.

Frankly, I don't believe it needed a Dave Sexton to come to the conclusion that the style encouraged by Tommy Docherty would have to be modified eventually, and I'm sure The Doc would have done this himself, had he remained manager. We had bounced back to the First Division, we had bounced on to Wembley; and this all-action, attacking style was not only refreshing to see, but it provided exciting football for the fans. Yet, eventually, other teams would have twigged us, and worked out their counters.

Players such as Gerry Francis, Dave Clement and John Hollins, whom Dave Sexton had left behind at Queen's Park Rangers, were unanimous in their opinion that Manchester United were getting one of the top men in the game when they appointed Dave Sexton.

How did they see him? – 'The most original coach I have ever known,' said Dave Clement. 'There is no-one better at getting the best out of a side so that it plays to its strengths,' said Gerry Francis. 'Almost everything I have achieved as a player, I owe to him,' said John Hollins.

And Peter Bonetti made a couple of points. 'Dave is a great tactician, with a tremendous football brain . . . he's almost an introvert, who likes to get on with the job without any glamour or publicity.'

I don't think Dave Sexton realised that he would have to be prepared to cope with so much publicity in his new job, or that he would find himself so much in a goldfish-bowl-like situation, when he first became Manchester United's manager. But I know that he came to realise this is one of the added pressures of the job, and he showed that he had acknowledged the fact, when things were not going too well, for he didn't duck any issues at that time.

But, generally speaking, he keeps his feelings to himself, preferring to let his actions and the way his team plays speak for him. And he certainly has his own ideas about how he wants a team to play. He doesn't want kick-and-rush stuff; he wants polished football – but with a bit of steel. He's studied football the world over, and he wants the best of British and the best of what the rest of the world has to offer. A tall order, and it takes time . . .

I think that during our run to Wembley in 1979 we began to display something of the style Dave Sexton had been patiently seeking – the ability to produce good attacking moves, while not forgetting defensive duties, and that touch of steel essential for success when the chips are down.

I have no doubt that Dave Sexton is happiest when he is putting his ideas into practice, mixing with players rather than being a public figure, and while he is prepared to go on television or be interviewed, I believe he would prefer to shun the limelight and concentrate on the mechanics of the job he's being paid to do.

So far, I haven't seen or heard him bawling out anyone at Old Trafford, though now and again, when he has been determined to make a point, there has been an edge to his tone, even if the words have been spoken quietly. If Dave Sexton ever did explode, in typical Tommy Docherty manner, I reckon the very foundations of Old Trafford would crumble from the shock.

I love the story told about him when he was in charge at Queen's Park Rangers, and during one game Dave Sexton pulled off Stan Bowles. Outwardly, the manager remained unmoved, as he ordered the substitution to be made; but he followed Stan Bowles to the dressing-room, and – just between the two of them – he poured forth his exasperation which was capsuled into half a dozen words: 'Stanley – you played like a drain!'

Anyone who begins to question Dave Sexton's strength – and I'm not referring to physical power, for his father was a renowned middleweight boxer and he knows all about the fight game – might care to consider that in changing the style of United's team, he stuck out his neck by spending almost two million pounds on four players.

He followed the Shankly maxim of going 'straight down the middle' when he signed Gordon McQueen and Joe Jordan; he landed Ray Wilkins from Chelsea; and he made his own decisions when it came to selling Stuart Pearson and Gordon Hill, as well as signing Mickey Thomas. And he knew full well that in letting Stuart and Gordon go, he was risking the wrath of United supporters – especially those who had been members of the Gordon Hill fan club.

That touch of steel I mentioned applies to Dave Sexton in no small degree, for in his dealings over Gordon McQueen and Ray Wilkins, he had to match clubs who were not disposed to let the players go cheaply. Leeds held out for a considerable time, as did Chelsea, and United's manager played the waiting game, too, as he endeavoured to secure two top stars for the kind of cash he was prepared to pay.

With Stuart Pearson, he offered the striker a new contract and, when it was rejected, made it clear that nothing better would be forthcoming. The way the new manager saw it, Stuart could re-sign, for improved terms, and if that didn't suit, it was his privilege to look for something better elsewhere.

In Gordon's case, Dave Sexton made up his mind that he wanted to add something extra to the team effort, and he decided that Mickey Thomas would provide the ingredient. It meant that Gordon became expendable, so far as United's manager was concerned, and he carried through the transfer in the face of opposition from a section of the fans.

I'm not taking sides . . . merely trying to show that when the chips are down, Dave Sexton has demonstrated that he is prepared to be his own man and back his judgement, showing patience and determination in his efforts to build the team he believes will bring the club success.

And if success is the standard by which Manchester United – and, consequently, their manager – must be judged, then it is as well to remember, also, that even before Dave Sexton had set foot inside Old Trafford, he had accomplished something in football.

When he was manager of Chelsea, he steered the Stamford Bridge club to honours – they won the F.A. Cup in 1970 and the European Cup-winners Cup the following year. I wonder if Dave Sexton ever imagined, on the night of the 1970 F.A. Cup final replay against Leeds at Old Trafford, that seven years on he would be back . . . as Manchester United's new manager?

After he had left Chelsea, he took over what was really an ailing team at Queen's Park Rangers, and he very nearly turned the side into a League championship winning outfit a few seasons ago. Indeed although Liverpool pipped Rangers by a point for the title, and Manchester United were not far behind, many people around the country gave their vote to Queen's Park Rangers as the team that had provided the most entertaining football.

And if Dave Sexton has enjoyed the good life on many occasions during his soccer career, he has also seen the other side of the picture, because at the beginning of 1962 it was a knee injury which forced him to hang up his boots as a player, and I can understand just what this must have meant to him, because of the worries I had about my own career after I was injured in the car crash. You have to be mentally tough to take blows like that and come back smiling.

Pleasant and relaxed though Dave Sexton's style may be, he can become tense when a big game is looming, yet he does his utmost to send his players out exuding confidence, and he has commanded respect and 100 per cent effort from the men at Manchester United.

Colchester manager Bobby Roberts, whose side lost to us in the fifth round of the F.A. Cup when we went to Wembley in 1979, made an interesting point about Dave Sexton just before we tackled Arsenal in the final, when he said that while he felt his own side had been worth a draw when they met United, he had to give us credit 'for the way they came down to our level and competed.'

Significantly, he added: 'Our only chance of beating them was for them to be complacent, but Dave Sexton had clearly told them they would have to get stuck in. I haven't seen that sort of commitment since 1970 when Chelsea – managed by Sexton – beat Leeds in the F.A. Cup-final replay.'

Yes, there's a streak of steel in Dave Sexton's make-up, and it showed during his days as manager of Chelsea, for he had his problems there, as well as his successes. I don't pretend to know just what went on behind the scenes at Stamford Bridge, but I do know that when there were problems on the playing side, Dave Sexton wouldn't compromise on an issue where he felt he was right – and he sold the talented, but temperamental, Alan Hudson and Peter Osgood as he made it plain that he was not prepared to give way.

United's manager almost pulled off a hat-trick of successes, too, at Chelsea, for after they had won the F.A. Cup and the European Cup-winners Cup in successive seasons, only Stoke City's 2–1 victory at Wembley in 1972 prevented Chelsea carrying off the Football League Cup.

I honestly believe that Dave Sexton came to Old Trafford

with his own ideas about the kind of team he wanted, and if they differed somewhat – but not all that much – from the ideas of his predecessor, he hoped to make it a quiet revolution, as befitted his personal style.

No-one appreciated more than the manager that through the years, United had gained fame because they had had a succession of outstanding individual stars, and if you look at the signings he made, Gordon McQueen and Joe Jordan certainly came under the heading of big names.

But the emphasis has gradually been placed on controlled build-ups, rather than flamboyant, all-out attack, and the work-rate of the side is being channelled to a purpose, rather than in the crash-bang, uninhibited type of play which brought results during the previous regime. Under The Doc, Manchester United were shock troops who tore through the opposition; under Dave Sexton, the play has become less of a headlong rush for while the accent is still on pushing forward and setting problems for the opposition, we know there are times when we've got to react to the reins.

Indeed, it was Danny Blanchflower, another famous name to manage Chelsea, who put his finger on the difference between the old and the new United when he remarked that while we still had the tradition for playing attacking football, under Dave Sexton it was much more organised. They say that a team reflects the manager, and if our buccaneering style reflected the management of Tommy Docherty, then the current style reflects the character of Dave Sexton.

12 My United Team. . .

Manchester United have had some great teams through the years since the war: there was the side which won the F.A. Cup in 1948; the side which, originally titled Busby's Babes, grew to greatness during the 1950's and (until the Munich air disaster decimated the team) threatened to carry off every honour in sight; there was the side which won the F.A. Cup in 1963; the side which captured the European Cup in 1968; and – in my time at Old Trafford – the side which went to Wembley three times in the space of four years, though there were some changes in personnel between 1976 and 1979.

As the last of the original Busby Babes, I've not only served under five managers at Manchester United, but seen and played alongside some famous names during the past 10 years or more, and many a time people ask me which is the side in which I would most like to have played. In other words, to choose my best Manchester United eleven (or, rather 10) from the players I have known. That, of course, lets out a host of famous names from the past . . . Johnny Carey, Jack Rowley, Stan Pearson, Charlie Mitten, Harry Gregg, Duncan Edwards, Roger Byrne, Eddie Colman, Tommy Taylor, Dennis Viollet, Liam Whelan. And those are just a few of United's stars of yesteryear.

In my era, I suppose I could include Bill Foulkes and one or two other players who were just about coming to the close of their days as stars with Manchester United, and again, Paddy Crerand would be on such a list. I have always felt that I owed something to Paddy, for when I arrived at Old Trafford as a raw, impressionable kid, standing somewhat in awe of the great names around me, he seemed to be the one who took most notice of me – possibly because, by then, he was also doing some work on the backroom side with the junior players, and I was one of them.

Certainly he gave me a great deal of helpful advice, and I can remember the times I almost blushed when I heard him saying some nice things about me. In those days, Bobby Charlton seemed to be a rather aloof figure, for he never talked a lot, and it was only after I had got to know him considerably better, as a team-mate, that I revised my original opinion. Then, I came to appreciate his ability not only as a team-mate, but to admire the personal qualities he brought to the game and to his attitude to life.

One thing I have learned during my years in professional football is that while the aim is for 11 individuals to play as a team, each man is different when it comes to personality, and you get the jokers and the quiet ones, the players who seem always to be together, and the ones who, by their nature, tend to be loners. Sometimes, even, you find yourself thinking you don't particularly like a player – and maybe he thinks the same about you – but when you pull on the red jersey, you accept that no matter which 11 men go out on the park, they are ready to function as a team. That's the way trophies are won and success is achieved.

I suspect that Harry Gregg would have been my choice for goalkeeper, if he'd still been playing for United when I arrived, and my thinking is probably influenced by the fact that he's a fellow-Irishman, and by the reputation he had earned as a player and the knowledge I have gained of him since he returned to Old Trafford as specialist goalkeeper coach. Coming right up to the present, I don't think Gary Bailey would expect me to plump for him, because he is still a newcomer to top-class football, though I have seen him make swift progress over the past couple of seasons.

Alex Stepney was the man in possession when I arrived at Old Trafford, and he remained the first-team choice virtually right through the following decade – an impressive testimony in itself to his ability, as well as to the service he gave Manchester United. Alex was a great joker, as I have already mentioned, and I remember a pre-season trip to Belgrade during Tommy Docherty's reign when the United 'keeper put one across a team-mate, with the help of Lou Macari.

The Doc told us all to make sure that we were dressed up and waiting in the hotel at 7.30 prompt one evening, because we had been invited to a function. Little Lou decided that Gerry Daly and Paddy Roche, who were rooming together, could have the evening off – which meant locking them in their room. Paddy was resting in bed, Gerry happened to be in the bathroom when Lou and Alex Stepney sauntered into their room.

The key to the door was lying on the table beside Paddy, and Lou managed to sneak hold of it without arousing Paddy's suspicions. As Lou was talking to Paddy, Alex lifted the phone off the bedside table and quietly slipped out of the room, taking the phone with him. Lou reminded the two players about the 7.30 appointment, then sauntered out and locked the door.

When Paddy and Gerry were ready to go down at 7.30, they found they couldn't get out of the room, and they couldn't phone for anyone to let them out . . . and in the corridor, team-mates were falling about laughing as they listened to the pair of them discussing their plight inside. And when Paddy and Gerry failed to put in an appearance on time, Tommy Docherty said : 'Right, that's it – we're off.'

Mind you, Alex didn't always have the final laugh; sometimes the joke rebounded on him. And in one particular instance it was costly for Manchester United, because during a derby game against Manchester City Alex called for the ball and Jimmy Nicholl promptly obliged . . . for as the 'keeper came off his line, Jimmy headed the ball towards Alex, and it sailed over his head and into the net. We lost that match 3–1 at Maine Road, and I can tell you Alex wasn't too pleased about that own-goal header from his team-mate.

Alex must get my vote for the goalkeeping position, for during close on 500 games for United he played consistently well, and even after he had apparently lost his first-team place at last to Paddy Roche he came back to prove The Doc wrong. Apart from the ability standpoint, one thing is essential – that the back-four players must have confidence in their last line of defence, and certainly Alex Stepney inspired such confidence. Indeed, I can remember a Cup-tie when Alex was doubtful about being able to play, because he had ricked his back. The news was kept quiet, though Paddy Roche was on standby, but Alex declared himself fit at the 11th hour and he played his usual consistent game.

I think, too, that he was a little bit unlucky in not being involved more at representative level, for in my book he was good enough to play regularly for England, as well as for United. And there wasn't much to choose between him and 'keepers like Ray Clemence, Peter Shilton and Joe Corrigan.

There are quite a few candidates for the right-back position, and if Bill Foulkes had still been at his peak probably he would have been my No. 1 choice. As it is, I have to leave Bill out of my considerations, since he had virtually finished as a player when I joined United. At that time, a youngster called John Fitzpatrick was making his way, and he impressed me as a good tackler and as a player who could pass the ball accurately. Those are two prime considerations when it comes to assessing full-backs, for you're not looking just for a man who can give the ball the boot.

Since 'Fitz' had his career curtailed by injury, United have had various other payers in his position – Brian Greenhoff did well in the No. 2 shirt, Alex Forsyth and Jimmy Nicholl had a real tussle for possession before Jimmy finally clinched a regular place, and all the players I have named could stake a claim for inclusion in my team.

But I cannot help harking back to John Fitzpatrick when it comes to making the final choice, and I reckon I'm influenced because of the fact that, to put it bluntly, wingers were scared of facing him. He was to United what Tommy Smith was to Liverpool, in his hey-day at Anfield – and, like Smithy, 'Fitz' could turn on some quality football. He wasn't just a clogger, though he could dish it out and take it.

John Fitzpatrick was tigerish in his tackling, and so many wingers took a dive when they came up against him that it wasn't surprising referees were kidded – with the result that United's right-back got his name in the book more often than should have been the case. For me, it was a tragedy when John Fitzpatrick had to hang up his boots when he should have been able to look forward to years of top-class football. And it was Manchester United's loss, for sure.

Left-back? – Despite the claims of Arthur Albiston and the admiration I have for Stewart Houston – who, at £40,000, must have represented one of the best buys of all time – I have no hesitation in naming Tony Dunne. Arthur and Stewart have graced the No. 3 jersey, and they have followed some big names . . . Roger Byrne and Noel Cantwell, for instance . . . but Tony was a first-team regular for so long that I have to go for him.

Possibly Stewart has been unlucky in his time at Old Trafford, for not only has he had to double as a central defender (and made a good job of it), but he has also been hampered by injuries which, almost certainly, didn't help him to become an automatic choice. His bad luck was Arthur's good fortune because, when we played Liverpool in the 1976 final, Arthur got his big chance, at 19. It was a fairy-tale experience for him when he was drafted into United's Cup-final side two weeks before Wembley and he stayed there.

Injury robbed Stewart of a place in 1976 just as in 1979 injury prevented him from staking a claim again, and Arthur was pitched in at the deep end against Liverpool. He hadn't even been involved in United's Cup run up to the final, and many people suspected that on the day, he would prove to be the weak link in United's defence, as Liverpool exploited his inexperience. But as it turned out, he was one of United's big successes, and by 1979 he was in the side as first choice at left-back.

Like Stewart, he had come through a few trials and tribulations – he'd been dropped, switched and seen his name linked with talk of a transfer – but he came through it all, and I feel that he is good enough to stay at the top for years to come. One day, he might even have totalled as many games for United as Tony Dunne did.

Tony was no chicken when I arrived at Old Trafford, but he was still proving to everyone that he could command a regular first-team place, and apart from his unquestioned ability as a footballer, he had the speed which could still enable him to catch an opponent and win back the ball after he had been beaten once.

A regular choice for the Republic of Ireland international side, Tony could scarcely be faulted, and his anticipation was so good that few forwards – and he was giving many of them a few years – found that they had the chance to get past him even once, in a direct confrontation. And when United finally decided that they must turn to someone else for the left-back position, Tony Dunne showed that as a free-transfer man he was a bargain when he made the short move to Bolton, for he won a promotion medal with them, and finished up playing a season of First Division football again before finally taking up a backroom job at Burnden Park.

When it comes to picking out two men to play at the heart of the defence, there are more than a few candidates, because in my years at Old Trafford I've seen players such as Ian Ure, Jim Holton, David Sadler, Brian Greenhoff, Martin Buchan and Gordon McQueen in action, while Stewart Houston has also been drafted in, during emergencies. I could even consider Bill Foulkes, and possibly if I had seen him as a team-mate over a lengthy spell – especially during his earlier days – I would have had no hesitation in naming him as one of my choices for a place in the middle of the back-four line.

The field can be narrowed down to three men, when it comes to looking for a recognised centre-half : Ian Ure, Jim Holton and Gordon McQueen. And for the man to play alongside, I have to choose between Brian Greenhoff, David Sadler and Martin Buchan.

Probably Brian was a bit unlucky in that he was switched around so much during his time with United, and it says a great deal for his ability that he still claimed England caps and did an effective job wherever he played. David Sadler also showed that he was an adaptable player, for he arrived at Old Trafford from Maidstone as a centre-forward with a reputation for scoring a lot of goals, and wound up playing at wing-half on occasion but generally in the middle of the back-four line, doing a similar job to Martin Buchan in that he played alongside the recognised centre-half.

However, in the long run, I settled for Martin Buchan, though I was reluctant to dismiss the claims of Brian Greenhoff. The fact is that I've seen so much of what Martin can do, and the influence he can exert on the team, let alone the defence, that the best tribute I can pay him is to say he is the complete footballer, and his reading of situations is almost uncanny. He can and does cover for the centre-half or either of the full-backs, as he sees the game developing; his play bears the stamp of authority, and almost clinical coolness; and he is the epitome of the team man.

In picking his partner I have to choose between Ian Ure, Jim Holton and Gordon McQueen – and that's not as easy as you might think, although I can whittle down the short list to two, without any disrespect to Ian Ure. When Ian was playing for Arsenal, he and Denis Law had some tremendous tussles against each other, and they always seemed to enjoy having a go, though they got on well enough when they became team-mates at Old Trafford.

Ian was a craggy stopper, not exceptionally mobile, but a solid barrier to get past. At the same time, when he joined Manchester United he was coming towards the close of his top-class career, and he had only something like half a season in United's first team. So, all things considered, this leaves me with room to manoeuvre, and concentrate on Jim and Gordon.

Jim's career has taken several surprising twists and turns, for he was given a free transfer by West Brom, given a chance to make it with Shrewsbury in the lower divisions, groomed by Harry Gregg (then managing Shrewsbury) for stardom, and recommended to Manchester United. Tommy Docherty made one of his famous quick decisions, an £80,000 fee changed hands – and Jim Holton swiftly became an idol of the Old Trafford faithful.

'Six foot two, eyes of blue, big Jim Holton's after you . . .' So chanted the fans, and car stickers proclaimed the message around Manchester and beyond. Off the field, Jim is a gentle giant; and on it, he's not the wild man some folk would have had you believe. Good in the air, solid as a rock, occasionally he would fall foul of referees because he caught an opponent who was getting past him. But there was never malice aforethought in Jim's tackle . . . just a determination to stop someone scoring a goal against United.

Jim graduated to the ranks of the Scottish internationals at Old Trafford, and his career seemed set for a good few years at the top with United. Then he broke a leg, spent some months making a recovery – and suffered another fracture. By the time he was staking his claims for a regular first-team spot again, the accent had changed, with Brian Greenhoff the man in possession.

It was a situation which, eventually, Jim found he couldn't accept, for he came to the conclusion that it was going to be impossible to break back into First Division football with Manchester United. So he indicated that he was ready to move on, and Sunderland signed him. Then, after a few months at Roker Park (during which there was a change of managers), he joined Coventry. I had, and still do have, a lot of time for big Jim, and he runs Gordon McQueen close. But alongside Martin Buchan I finally plumped for the man from Leeds . . . even if he does have a tendency now and then to think he's playing in attack !

I'm not dismissing Gordon's all-round ability, or the fact that he can score some valuable goals, especially when he goes up for set pieces; but I think Jock Stein got it right when he said that Gordon's job was to win the ball in defence and give it – and when he's concentrating on that job, for me he's the best in the business.

So now I come to the midfield section, and I'm picking myself on the left-hand side of the park. At first, when I joined United and scored some rapid goals, people reckoned that I was going to become a striker with the scoring touch; but I never really felt, deep down, that this would turn out to be the case. Indeed, I never wanted to be a striker – I always believed that eventually my best position would turn out to be in midfield, where I could play creative football and, given the chance, make the odd break and stick the ball in the net.

I'll say straight away that my two midfield partners would be Paddy Crerand and Bobby Charlton, for though there could be other contenders such as Nobby Stiles, Lou Macari, Francis Burns, Alan Gowling, Gerry Daly and Brian Greenhoff, my two nominees were the aces. Paddy was never a racehorse, but he made the ball do the work in such a manner that pace wasn't a prime qualification – he saw moves before they were on, anticipated where the ball would be, and could spray passes to any part of the field. When Paddy was on song, United were on song; he made the midfield tick, and he was a creative artist.

So was Bobby Charlton, who also packed a blistering shot. And, like Paddy, Bobby was a tremendous competitor – he wanted to win in five-a-side games every bit as much as he wanted to win matches where points were at stake. If his side was losing, he would be shouting and urging everyone to put their backs into it. When he played deep, he used his passing ability to send a long raking ball from one side of the park to the other.

He also scored a lot of goals for his club and his country – though I still maintain that if Bobby had got into the 18-yard box more often his explosive finishing power would have brought him many more goals. I remember him scoring two tremendous goals in the 1966 World Cup against Mexico, and even today, whenever I see a player hammer one in from 25 to 30 yards, it reminds me of Bobby's lethal finishing power.

My front line – inevitably – brings me to George Best, and he goes in automatically. For he is the first name on the list. During his hey-day at United, thousands of words were written about George and his supreme footballing ability, and it doesn't really need me to remind anyone who saw him in action that here was a player who had the lot. He could beat a man so easily, he could win the ball in a tackle; he could open up the way for team-mates, and he could rifle goals himself. He had skill and courage, and some of the moves he produced were little short of magical. For me, Best was the best.

It's when I come to the other two front men that I have to think a bit harder, for I've played alongside some great footballers with United. I'm just grateful that I've been able to slot Bobby Charlton into a midfield role, otherwise the choice up front would have been even more difficult, for names that trip off the tongue include Denis Law, Brian Kidd, Jimmy Greenhoff, Stuart Pearson, Steve Coppell (and he could have been a candidate for midfield) and Joe Jordan.

At the end of the day, I decided that Stuart Pearson and Jimmy Greenhoff should be the men to partner George Best – then I thought about it again, and changed my mind. Much as I admire Jimmy's sharpness and scoring instinct, somehow my mind kept turning back to the blond-haired Scot who was a star when I was still a newcomer at United. And finally, I decided Denis Law must go in.

So I had to revise my team and delete the name of my original substitute – for the second time. At first, having settled for an attacking trio of Best, Pearson and Greenhoff, I pencilled in the name of Steve Coppell as substitute. Then I decided that Lou Macari should be 12th man. Then I thought again, and – having replaced Jimmy Greenhoff by Denis Law – I felt it only fair to give Jimmy the substitute's spot.

So there's my all-star side: Alex Stepney; John Fitzpatrick, Martin Buchan, Gordon McQueen, Tony Dunne; Paddy Crerand, Bobby Charlton, Sammy McIlroy; George Best, Stuart Pearson, Denis Law. Substitute: Jimmy Greenhoff.

I plumped for Denis because he always had that essential attribute for a striker – he'd go in where angels feared to tread. And apart from that special finishing ability he possessed, you need courage when the boots are flying in the box. The same goes for Stuart Pearson, with whom I struck up a good understanding in quick time after he was signed from Hull. Stuart has suffered more than his fair share of injuries during his career, but he's proved that apart from his ability, he's no coward. I know, because he certainly took a lot of weight off me when we were operating together in the front line.

Having picked my all-star Manchester United side, I'll just add that I would have loved to play in the United team of the early 1960's – around 1963, when I was nine or ten years old. That was when I first began to take a real interest in football, and it seemed to me that United's team then had the lot. It included Tony Dunne, Bill Foulkes, Bobby Charlton, Paddy Crerand and Denis Law, And for good measure there were names like Harry Gregg, Maurice Setters, Noel Cantwell, Albert Quixall, David Herd and Johnny Giles.

Maybe you'll disagree with my all-star team, and that's your privilege – if I'd been older, I'd probably have been even more hard pressed to pick 11 names out of the galaxy of stars who wore United's colours during the past three or four decades. But I reckon you'll give me credit for having named a side which could match up to the most demanding requirements, and I think it would take something special to beat the line-up I've named.

13 My United Team-Mates

In little more than four years, during the early part of the
1970's, Manchester United signed more than a dozen players,
at a total cost of around one and three quarters of a million
pounds. It made the £116,000 the club had paid for Denis
Law seem modest, as United spashed £200,000 apiece on
Ted MacDougall, Lou Macari and Ian Moore, fees ranging
between £100,000 and £160,000 on Stuart Pearson, Martin
Buchan, George Graham, Jimmy Greenhoff and Alex Forsyth.
And in addition, United recruited Jim Holton, Stewart
Houston, Gordon Hill, Jim McCalliog and Steve Coppell.

In March, 1972, United spent £400,000; between Sept-
ember and the end of that year, they had invested another
£540,000; in January, 1973, United forked out another
£280,000; and so the spending spree went on. But if we all
thought that such massive outlays then were staggering, we've
now learned to come to terms with a situation where zip
goes a million on one player alone. And Manchester United
have set new records for the club when it comes to buying
in the transfer market.

I sometimes wonder what Harry Gregg thinks, when he
looks around him at Old Trafford now and ponders on the
way that transfer fees have escalated since the day he arrived
as a star player. When he signed for the club at the end of
1957, Doncaster Rovers received £23,500 from Manchester
United – and that was a world-record fee for a goalkeeper at
the time. Furthermore, there wasn't a clause which said a
player should receive five per cent cut of the fee, even if
Harry's share would have been a modest £1,175. Now Harry
is working daily with players who have cost fees ranging from
a mere £200,000 to more than three-quarters of a million
pounds – apiece.

What do I think about the way transfer fees have spiralled? – Well, even allowing for inflation, I must confess that a fee of a million and a half pounds strikes me as being – in a word – ridiculous. But then, I'm not a manager who has to barter in a market which is governed very much by the law of supply and demand.

Nevertheless, although I rate big-money buys such as Steve Daley, Andy Gray and Trevor Francis very good players indeed, I think I'm making a valid point when I ask . . . just how much would George Best be worth, if he were at his peak and starring for Manchester United today?

Another question : will football be able to retreat from that £1,500,000 landmark? – I don't think so. We didn't really believe that the day would ever dawn when an English club would pay such a vast amount of money for one player, but I'll tell you something – even while this book was being written, the record fee shot up from £1M to £1,500,000 and I had to revise my own ideas pretty quickly. Now, I reckon few people would be sceptical when I suggest that if the rate of inflation in football continues, we shall see £2,000,000 changing hands before too long – if it hasn't already done so. Unless, of course, the clubs do something to put a ceiling on transfer deals.

I cost Manchester United nothing, and there are times I'm grateful for that. Mickey Thomas cost the club £330,000, and he admitted that it made him feel nervous when he thought about the transfer price-tag which had been put on him. If he felt nervous about £330,000, what would a £1,500,000 fee have done to him? – I have my doubts that he would have been able to walk out on the pitch . . . and I have a shrewd suspicion that United's record-priced signing, Ray Wilkins, was affected initially, also, by the £800,000-plus price tag which was hung around his neck when he left Stamford Bridge for Old Trafford. Certainly his early games tended to be quiet, almost as if he were afraid of putting a foot wrong.

The economics of professional football take some understanding, at times, for it is no secret that many clubs in the League have been struggling to survive – or, at least, pay their way – for years. The transfer market has provided a lifeline for many clubs when they have produced players who have made the grade, while other, wealthy clubs have creamed off the top talent.

I guess I would love to pick up a five per cent cut of a £1,500,000 transfer fee, but I believe that being involved in a big-money deal must bring its problems for players. They can and do argue that they don't fix the fee, so they aren't going to let it worry them, but I know from my own experience that when your form begins to suffer, you worry any way – whether you've cost a big transfer fee or not.

I suffered from a lean spell during the months it took me to recover from the car crash, and I had to work hard at getting fit and regaining form. It would have been much more difficult for me if I'd cost a huge transfer fee and found the fans were getting on my back because I was going through a lean spell – and that happens to every player at some time or another. Just as you can hit a purple patch, so you can suffer a loss of form. Having said that, I don't think I would have sleepless nights now if I'd cost, say, £400,000 in the transfer market, because the million-pound-plus standard has now been set. If I'd cost a million, I'd start to worry then!

In most things, you can assess the value of an article: but in football, there are always the intangibles – and sometimes a player who isn't valued highly, in terms of cash, suddenly becomes a very valuable property indeed. There have been instances in reverse, too, where a player had a big fee placed on him one minute, and the next minute something had happened to change the whole course of the proposed deal.

I'm thinking now of the dramatic change in fortunes for two players who virtually found their whole world changing in quick time. One is Gary Bailey, the other is Jim Blyth.

Manchester United were on the point of paying Coventry City something like £400,000 to sign the Scots 'keeper, and Gary was then an unknown youngster trying to gain a foothold in professional football here. But instead of Jim Blyth signing for United, he was on his way back to Highfield Road

E

after a medical examination had gone against him. For Blyth, that must have appeared like a tragedy; for Gary Bailey, the failure of this big-money deal to materialise was the signal for a swift, upward trend in his own fortunes.

United pitched Gary in at the deep end, for a First Division game at Old Trafford against Ipswich Town, the club for which his father, Roy, had once played. And the lad from South Africa stayed in United's side right through the season, collecting England Under-21 honours and winding up in our F.A. Cup-final team at Wembley.

I've taken more than a passing interest in Gary's progress, because as it happened I was just about the first United player he met, for I sat beside him on a train journey back from London, after we had played in a game there. I hadn't a clue as to the identity of this tall blond-haired youngster, then he told me that he had arrived for a month's trial at Old Trafford. Frankly, I expected to see him around for a few weeks, and then the chances were that he would be on his way.

He told me that he had been given the chance to show his paces at Ipswich and at Crystal Palace, but 'I fancy United'. And so he came to be sitting on the train, having been invited to travel back with the team after the match. However, he didn't train with the senior players, so the next I saw of him was when he got a chance to show what he could do in the reserves.

Suddenly, he was making his debut against Ipswich, and coming through it without having conceded a goal. It was one of those afternoons when the ground was greasy, and these conditions make handling the ball a nightmare for a 'keeper, so Gary prepared as thoroughly as he could by dipping a ball into a tub of water before the game and getting the feel of it. And he did sufficient to impress everyone in the match itself.

I've got to know him considerably better since our initial meeting on the train from London, and it's possible now to assess his chances of making it to the top and staying there. He's sure of himself, without being cocky, and as the season progressed the defenders grew more confident about leaving things to him. So by the time he played at Wembley he knew that he had a good chance of becoming recognised as a top-flight 'keeper, and that all he needed was experience.

Gary has a great physique for a goalkeeper, and he's brave and agile. He also has something else going for him – the expert knowledge of Harry Gregg, who has seen and done it all in his own time as a 'keeper. Gary believes in Harry 100 per cent, and Harry is honest enough to tell Gary if he's making mistakes. Harry has helped other goalkeepers in his time – Joe Corrigan, Dai Davies, Jimmy Rimmer, John Phillips – and Gary has the intelligence to appreciate that United's specialist goalkeeper coach can show him the way to the top.

It takes all sorts to make a world and, of course, there are different personalities in every football team. Undoubtedly one of the strongest personalities at Manchester United is Martin Buchan, and he has been a key man in defence for the club ever since he arrived from Aberdeen. Martin takes a bit of getting to know; but once you do know him, he commands your respect.

Jimmy Greenhoff once said that Martin didn't mind whom he offended, if he felt he was in the right. 'He'll let the whole stadium know', said Jimmy. And he will, as Gordon Hill discovered when he got that cuff on the head from Martin during a game, after Gordon had failed to mark an opponent at a throw-in.

Martin could have gone to university, but he decided to follow his father as a professional footballer, and he became the youngest skipper Aberdeen had ever had. In 1970 he was leading them to victory over Celtic in the final of the Scottish Cup, and two years later he was moving south of the Border to Old Trafford, after having claimed the captaincy of Scotland's Under-23 team.

Frank O'Farrell signed him because he was looking for the sort of qualities that Martin possessed, but he didn't become captain of United until 1975, by which time Tommy Docherty was in charge at Old Trafford. The Doc has a pretty powerful personality, but the relationship between manager and skipper was never that of boss and yes-man, for Martin still said his piece when he felt the occasion called for it. And I'm sure Tommy Docherty respected Martin for this, even though he once claimed United's captain would argue that the ball was square, if The Doc said it was round.

If Martin Buchan sometimes gives the appearance of being imperious, his team-mates have learned to accept his style of leadership, and we know that he'll back us up when he believes we have a cause. He doesn't suffer fools easily, he can be abrasive in his manner and with words, but in the final analysis, he can usually make people understand what he's driving at, and why. And it's not often that he is wrong.

His partner in the centre of United's defence, Gordon McQueen, took time to settle into the side on his arrival from Leeds, and possibly the £500,000 transfer fee proved a bit of a burden initially.

Towards the end of 1978 and early in the New Year, Gordon was finding life a bit difficult, because he was coming in for some criticism – not all of it gentle – from people who reckoned that he wasn't living up to his reputation as a top centre-half. Indeed, his form suffered to the extent that he lost his place in the Scotland team, and Jock Stein said at the time that it was up to Gordon himself to put matters to rights.

It's to the big fellow's credit that he buckled down to the job, and his performances during the second half of the season were, in my opinion, one of the major factors in enabling United to reassert themselves and go marching to Wembley. Gordon and Joe Jordan are great pals, and they go through a pre-match warm-up routine together, then Gordon goes out into the corridor on his own to have a kickabout with a ball. Once the game begins, he knows his job is to stop the opposition from getting through – but he loves going up for set pieces, and has scored some valuable goals for us.

Joe is a tough guy with a heart of gold. He can present a fearsome sight when he's battling for the ball, but off the field he's one of the quiet men – almost gentle, in fact. I suppose the fearsome appearance stems from the fact that Joe has three front teeth missing, and he takes out his 'falsies' before a game. Joe lost two teeth when he made his debut for

Leeds, as he went boring into the 18-yard box looking for a goal. The ball came over, low, and as Joe dived to head it a boot connected with his mouth and two teeth went missing. It was a similar incident in a game against Southampton which cost him yet another tooth, though that time it was an opponent's head which caught him.

Joe had to convince the Old Trafford faithful that he was worth the £350,000 that United had paid Leeds for him, but he's never shirked a challenge in his life and, just as he goes in muck or nettles when the boots are flying, so he answered the challenge of the doubters when he joined United.

Both Joe and Gordon have had to discipline themselves during the past year or two, because they have known the problems of facing suspension. In fact, Joe kicked off his career at Old Trafford by not kicking off . . . because he arrived after having started a three-match ban; and Gordon took the long walk from pitch to dressing-room when he was sent off at Old Trafford during a League Cup-tie against Stockport. After having been elbowed in the mouth, he reacted by retaliating.

You have my word for it that, with all the good intentions in the world, it isn't easy to count to 10 when someone is having a go at you – and Joe and Gordon have taken a great deal of stick from opposition, because they have the courage to go in where it hurts. I think both players found it difficult when they arrived at Old Trafford, also, because the fans at Leeds didn't like it, and as Joe and Gordon were still living there and travelling over to Manchester for training, they felt the backlash of their respective transfers.

Indeed, Gordon had to get accustomed to receiving abusive letters and being called a traitor, and it must have been a worrying time for him when we crossed the Pennines to play at Elland Road for the first time since his move to Manchester. There was no fond welcome from the Leeds fans, but Gordon gave the best possible answer. He kept a tight rein on his tongue and his temper . . . and scored a goal as we beat his old team-mates.

Steve Coppell, too, has had his problems since he was signed by United from Tranmere Rovers. Nothing to do with temperament, but because the move split his family right down the middle. They're Liverpudlians, of course, and perhaps the worst time of all for Steve was when we played Liverpool in the semi-final of the F.A. Cup in 1979, for he knew that while some members of the family wanted United to win, brother Kevin, especially, was still rooting for Liverpool. And, of course, as a youngster Steve supported the Anfield Reds.

Steve, who signed for United while he was still studying at university, has graduated to England-international status, and he became an overnight success when he was given his chance in the first team. He also learned something in quick time, as we all did, when United played Juventus in Europe and found opponents standing on his toes and poking fingers in his eyes. Steve isn't a vindictive person, but he said later that when Juventus were competing in the European Cup, he wanted them to reach the final . . . just so that he could have the pleasure of seeing Liverpool humiliate them at Wembley. But it turned out to be Bruges whom Liverpool met there.

It's not often that you get two brothers playing for the same club, let alone in the First Division, but Brian and Jimmy Greenhoff made it a double when the latter signed for United from Stoke. They had come a long way from the cobbled streets of Barnsley where they first learned to kick a ball around.

Their dad was a footballer with Lincoln City for a spell – he'd started off as a miner – and Jimmy was the first of the brothers to sign professional forms, with Leeds. Then it was on to Birmingham, Stoke – where he won a League Cup medal in 1972 – and finally, Old Trafford, as a £120,000 transfer fee changed hands.

Brian might just have become a cricketer with Yorkshire – he won a county cap at schoolboy level – but once he took over the No. 4 jersey brother Jimmy had worn in the town schools' Soccer team it was football all the way. And when Jimmy played in the Leeds side that beat Arsenal in the 1968 League Cup final, Brian was one of the Wembley ball boys picked by the Barnsley Schools Football Association.

At the time, as Brian saluted Jimmy on the running track, after Leeds had won, the elder brother passed a comment which was to prove prophetic 'Brian could be back here as a player himself one day.' And in the spring of 1977, the brothers played together in the Manchester United side which beat Liverpool in the F.A. Cup final.

Tommy Docherty was in luck's way when he signed Jimmy – and lucky again that Brian was at Old Trafford when he took over, for as manager of Rotherham he had tried to land the younger Greenhoff for the Millmoor club, and failed. Jimmy is one of the sharpest strikers I've known, for he sizes up situations in a flash, and can tuck away a half-chance before the 'keeper is alert to the danger. As for Brian, he's proved one of the most versatile players in top-flight football, and deserved the international honours he has won with England.

So far as I am concerned, Brian had nothing to prove when he left Old Trafford for Leeds at the start of season 1979–80. He played for Manchester United at right-back, in the centre of the defence, in midfield and up front, and it's difficult to say which of the two positions – central defender or midfield man – is his best. But there's no doubt that wherever he plays, he brings to his game not only creative ability, but a readiness to work and help his team-mates – and, like his brother, he's no mug at sticking away scoring chances.

Which brings me to Stuart Pearson, one of the unluckiest players I've known during my time at Old Trafford, for I'm sure he would have collected a lot more caps with England if he hadn't suffered so many injury problems. I struck up a good understanding with Stuart soon after he signed for United, and I know how much he helped me with his unselfish play. Then he looked set to forge a partnership alongside Joe Jordan . . . until the injury jinx really struck him down.

His left knee began to play him up when he was leading the England attack at Wembley in a game against Hungary, and though he went on tour afterwards with United to the US, the knee caused further problems. The sequel was a cartilage operation, and that seemed to be the end of the matter – until a blood clot on the knee caused complications, and that meant Stuart had to stay off the leg for almost a fortnight.

Further treatment in hospital was necessary, and then Stuart had a spell on crutches, though he was able to do some body weights to keep himself in trim, but in the end season 1978–79 couldn't finish soon enough for him, because it had turned out to be more or less a non-event, in spite of the fact that United had gone to Wembley, for Stuart Pearson was just one of the 100,000 onlookers.

There followed a dispute with the club about the new contract he had been offered, for Stuart felt unable to accept the terms and it was made clear that it was entirely up to him – which, of course, brought speculation about a transfer from Old Trafford. That speculation was heightened as clubs such as Chelsea, West Brom, West Ham, Sunderland and Queen's Park Rangers developed a definite interest in United's striker. Finally, on the eve of the new season, Stuart made his move, as he signed for West Ham . . . and went to Wembley with the Hammers for the 1980 F.A. Cup final against Arsenal.

Around the same time, there was also a question mark about the future of defender Stewart Houston, another of the unfortunate injury brigade at Old Trafford, and here again, there was talk of a possible move, first to Oldham, then to Aston Villa. Having had my own worries about injuries a few years previously, I couldn't help but sympathise with two players who had been long-term casualties, and in Stewart Houston's case, he had missed the chance of appearing in two F.A. Cup finals.

It was at the beginning of May, 1977, that Stewart received the injury which put him out of the final against Liverpool, when he and Chris Garland both went for a high ball and Stewart landed awkwardly. At first, it seemed as if he had merely taken an uncomfortable knock, but when Alex Stepney came racing from his goal almost to the half-way line, where Stewart was lying, it became clear that something serious had happened.

Alex was signalling for the stretcher-bearers to get on the field straight-away, because he thought Stewart had broken an ankle, but medical examination showed there was no break – instead, the ankle had been dislocated, and Stewart had to have an operation on the ligaments, so he was out of action until the following season.

Injury dogged him in season 1978–79, too, and he had only just begun to challenge for a first-team spot by the time United were preparing for another final at Wembley, and time was too short for Stewart to hope to displace Arthur Albiston, so again he had to settle for a spectator's role. Some players never figure in a side which reaches Wembley, but when you do play for a club which goes to the F.A. Cup final twice, and you miss out each time, I think you can truly claim to have had more than your share of bad luck.

Stewart's career at Old Trafford came to its close in the spring of 1980, for United announced that at the end of the season they would be letting him go on a free transfer in a generous gesture to a player who had given them good service and shown himself to be a loyal clubman.

14 Soccer's Ups and Downs

Every professional footballer has times when it seems things can't go wrong, and other moments when nothing appears to go right. One of the things which gave me tremendous satisfaction was scoring a goal against Real Madrid, even though it was only in a friendly match; one of the worst misses of my career was in a match against Newcastle United; and two other games linger in the memory – one against Bristol City, when I received marching orders for the first time in my life, and one against Juventus, when United were competing in Europe.

The game against Real Madrid was a pre-season friendly, and Manchester United won it, 4–0. We were awarded a throw-in, and I took the throw, lobbing the ball to Jimmy Greenhoff, near the corner flag on the right-hand side of the field. He put the ball straight back to me, and I simply put my head down, raced through a few tackles, and hit the ball firmly with my left foot – straight into the net. It gave me great satisfaction to have scored against such renowned opposition.

It was another game at Old Trafford, against Newcastle, when I registered what I still regard as the worst miss of my career. Willie Morgan crossed the ball to me from the wing, and I was completely on my own, near the six-yard box. The 'keeper had stayed on his line, presumably because he expected me to hit a first-time shot – and I realised afterwards that I should have done. Instead, I brought the ball down and got it under control, and the Newcastle 'keeper decided it was time he took a hand in things, so he came racing out of his goal and rushed towards me.

I looked up, saw him coming, and – from five yards out – side-footed the ball past him. I had all the goal at which to aim . . . and what did I do? – I sliced the ball wide.

The sending-off incident came during a match when Manchester United were playing Bristol City and Gerry Gow and myself tangled. He caught me with his studs, and for a moment I saw red, so I retaliated while we were both still on the ground. When I got to my feet, the referee was holding up the red card, and I trudged sadly off the Ashton Gate pitch. Believe me, it's true what they say about it being a long and lonely walk to the dressing-room. But I'm pleased to say that Gerry Gow and I have both managed to avoid getting into a similar situation when we've been opponents since. That incident brought me a one-match suspension – and taught me a lesson, even if I got marching orders in another game, against Nottingham Forest, in season 1979–80.

I've had maybe half a dozen bookings during my career, as well, and they have all come about because I've retaliated or shouted the odds. If I've any excuse, it lies in the fact that during recent seasons referees have been consciously clamping down, in accordance with orders from above, so what would have brought just a 'watch it' warning before became an occasion for holding up the yellow card.

One incident which brought me a booking – and in the opening minutes – came when United were playing against Norwich, and I found myself being flattened. I jumped smartly to my feet and gave my opponent, Mick Maguire, a shove – and the referee wasted no time in producing the yellow card.

Once you've received a booking during a match, you know that the next offence is liable to bring marching orders, and while I don't think you consciously pull out of a tackle, you have to keep on reminding yourself that you cannot afford any more trouble, so maybe you're not quite as effective after that, because your concentration is divided between the action of the game and the knowledge that you must keep your temper, even when you're coming in for a bit of stick.

When we played Juventus in Italy, it's a wonder there weren't marching orders for a few of the United players, because we were provoked almost beyond endurance by the opposition. And I say that in all seriousness. When we played at Old Trafford, we beat Juventus 1–0, and it was crystal clear that they were out simply to stop us from adding to the score.

One of their Italian internationals was doing a marking job on me, and I'm not exaggerating when I say that during the game I found myself being spat upon and my shirt being tugged. Even when you tried to avoid him, you would find a kick being aimed at you.

In Italy, it was another of the international brigade who kept a close eye on me, and the business started in the first minute of the match. The ball was cleared up the park, and I was about to turn and see if I could get possession when I felt an elbow gouging into one of my eyes.

The atmosphere was horrific, with the Italian fans screaming their heads off, and what went on off the ball was incredible.

Stuart Pearson, Steve Coppell, myself – just about every United player came in for the treatment at one stage or another, and you felt as if you were taking your life in your hands whenever you ventured near the ball. Juventus gave us a 3–0 beating, and my feeling at the time was if this was what the U.E.F.A. Cup was all about, then I wasn't sorry to see the back of it. Certainly I wouldn't like to come up against opposition like that week in, week out.

I've played against other Continental teams – Ajax, St Etienne and Porto – in European competition, and I have to say that we fared better against such sides, for the most part, though there was trouble in the crowd when we met St Etienne in France. We were out on the pitch warming up and checking on whether we had the right studs in our boots for the conditions when suddenly we became aware of the police moving into a section of the crowd.

On closer inspection we realised that this was where some United fans were congregated, and in a matter of minutes the batons were flying and people were being hustled from the gound. You could hear people screaming, and it wasn't exactly a pretty sight or the most pleasant experience before the game had even begun.

However, we managed not to let such scenes affect us,

and the way we played against the crack French side was one of the finest team performances we have given during my time with United. It was only when the game was in its dying minutes that St Etienne managed to score a goal – and then it was an equaliser.

Some you win, some you lose and some you draw. I recall seeing the F.A. Charity Shield game between Manchester United and Tottenham Hotspur at Old Trafford at the start of season 1967–68, thanks to the wonder of television, and the result was 3–3. It was the day Brian Kidd made his bow for United and Bobby Charlton scored two goals with thunderbolt shots from outside the 18-yard box.

Pat Jennings got a goal, too – from a goal kick. It was a wet day, as I remember, and United's 'keeper Alex Stepney was standing out of his goal as the kick from his opposite number landed. The ball bounced just about on the 18-yard line . . . then skidded off the turf and went over the United man's head and into the net. As Alex went up, he got a finger-tip to the ball, but that didn't do him any good.

Mention of Brian Kidd reminds me of derby games against Manchester City, and there came a time when 'Kiddo', who had been United-daft and idolised by the Stretford Enders, was playing in the sky-blue of City and doing his level best to put one across United. In the earlier days, he'd revelled in the United-City feuding which used to precede a derby game.

Malcolm Allison used to gee his City men up and say outrageous things about the opposition, while 'Kiddo' used to say about City: 'Let's stuff them.' As time passed, a lot of the aggro disappeared, and much of the heat went out of the confrontations so that, for some of the players, at least, a derby occasion assumed the proportions of just another game.

There was a lot of needle at the time I made my derby-game debut, and it showed during the action, although when Franny Lee was awarded a penalty after Tommy O'Neil had tackled him it looked a blatant dive by the City man to me.

At any rate, Franny couldn't have had much more than his pride injured, for he got up and took the spot-kick himself. The way he'd gone down, you'd have thought he would have needed a stretcher to get him off the park. And now that it's all past history, I suspect that if you asked Franny now whether or not he went for a penalty, the answer would probably be 'Yes . . .' He had that penalty-area tumble off to a fine art; so much so that I believe referees were taken in sometimes as Franny ran full tilt at defenders and it needed only the slightest knock for him to go flying.

Once a spot-kick had been awarded, Franny Lee didn't give goalkeepers much of a chance; and mention of goalkeepers reminds me of one who never became a first-team regular at Old Trafford, but who was a real character. Willie Carrick hailed from Dublin, and if he couldn't sing like Josef Locke he could certainly warble in a style reminiscent of Andy Williams.

We had a youngster on trial one day, so Willie vacated his place between the sticks and asked if he could have a go up front. He did well enough to rattle in four goals for the A team that day.

Manchester City goalkeeper Joe Corrigan will remember me, too, I expect, for one goal I put past him. It happened in the derby game at Old Trafford after we had just lost the F.A. Cup final against Southampton in 1976, and none of the United players felt much like facing such keen opposition after the disappointment of that defeat at Wembley. But I cheered up myself and my team-mates as I made to go one way and put the ball past Joe into the opposite corner of the net with a left-footer. It's always that bit harder to score when the 'keeper comes out to meet you, and big Joe had done just this and spread himself. That was what made up my mind for me when it came to deciding where I was going to put the ball. And we won, 2–0.

I don't much like coming up against 'keepers of Joe Corrigan's calibre, and Peter Shilton is another who usually manages to perform minor miracles when he's playing against Manchester United. We haven't stuck many goals past him during my time at Old Trafford – although I suppose a lot of teams could say the same about Nottingham Forest's last line of defence.

One player for whom I had a great deal of time was

Alan Oakes, the defender who spent 14 years with Manchester City and who never gave of less than his best in hundreds of first-team matches. There was one derby game where United gave City a 3–1 beating, and Alan didn't mind it at all . . . because that was his testimonial match at Maine Road.

It poured down, that night; but it didn't stop 30,000 people for turning up to express their admiration for a player who had given top value for money right through the years – and I mean the fans' admission money, because Oakes didn't cost City a penny when he joined them. I'd like to think that one day, the players would line up for me and applaud as generously and genuinely as the United and City lads did for Alan Oakes that night.

If I need reminding about the ups and downs of football, I need hark back to just one season, when we made our best start for many a year. We lost only two matches – against Everton and Leeds United – before the Christmas, and by the turn of the year were sitting on top of the First Division with a five-point lead. That was in Frank O'Farrell's time as manager.

The New Year brought a totally different turn of events, for United suffered seven League defeats in successive matches –and the worst was a 5–1 hammering by Leeds United at Elland Road, where we have done so well on other occasions.

We finished eighth in the First Division, as we had done during the previous term, though we collected five more points. It was around that time that Martin Buchan joined United from Aberdeen for a fee of £125,000, and Ian Moore arrived as a £200,000 investment.

It was also around the time that George Best skipped training and was dropped and fined two weeks' wages by the club – and they ordered him to go back into digs after he had moved into a luxury house in the executive belt of Bramhall, in Cheshire. The close season brought another runaway episode, when George missed a tour game in Israel and revealed that he was turning his back on football.

He made his peace with the club again, took a two-week suspension, and for a time moved in with Paddy Crerand

and his family. In spite of all the problems George presented, he had still managed to end the season as Manchester United's leading marksman, with 18 goals in the League, five in the F.A. Cup, and three in the League Cup.

Meanwhile, he had been matched by Bobby Charlton when it came to first-team appearances, for both players totalled 40 League games and all the Cup-ties . . . and Bobby then was the veteran of the side and 34 years old. It became an open secret that Bobby and George didn't see eye to eye about the way George was running his football career, and eventually, during Tommy Docherty's reign at Old Trafford, George made his final exit from the club.

There came a time when I walked in to see The Doc and told him : 'I'd like to be dropped from the team – it's what I deserve, because I'm playing rubbish.' My action stemmed from a conviction that I wasn't being used to my best advantage in United's side. It was mid-September, 1976, and although I was playing in the front line, I hadn't scored even one goal.

Not only was I worried about my form; I had become increasingly convinced that my best position in the side was in midfield. It was a feeling I'd had for a long time – ever since people had started to stick that George Best label on me, in fact. It wasn't just a question of wanting to get away from that kind of image, but a matter of sorting out in my own mind where I was going. And the more I saw of Bobby Charlton, pinging the passes around from a deep position, the more I felt that this was what I would most like to do.

I've never been one of those players who tells his manager : 'If you don't let me operate in a certain position, I won't play for you.' I've always been amenable to discipline, and I've played in whichever position I've been selected . . . though there was an occasion when I asked to be given a different number when I was playing for Northern Ireland.

That was when, after having played for my country 11 times in the No. 10 jersey – and having failed to score even one goal – I asked if I could switch to the No. 8 shirt I usually wore in club matches, for a European championship game against Norway. But I still had to wait for my 13th appearance in an international match before I scored my first goal.

Going back to that conversation I had with Tommy Docherty, the motive behind my request to be dropped was twofold. First, the previous season I had been given a chance to show what I could do in a midfield role, when I played there as stand-in for Lou Macari; and I had enjoyed the experience and felt I had done well. Secondly, David McCreery and Alan Foggon, both front-line men, couldn't get into United's side while I was holding down a forward spot, and if I wasn't scoring goals, they were entitled to feel that one of them deserved a chance.

In a way, I deeply regretted that burst of goals when I had first got into the Manchester United team, for it encouraged people to think of me as a striker. But I had never looked upon myself as a regular marksman, even though I had totalled 13 goals one season and 10 in another. I judged myself on my international record – one goal . . . and at the time I asked Tommy Docherty to leave me out of United's side, I had made 17 appearances for Northern Ireland.

The Doc gave me a fair hearing, and he even agreed with me that midfield was my best position. But he also pointed out that the team was going well and that he wasn't prepared to drop someone else just so that I could feel happier about my own game. He was satisfied with the job I was doing up front, and I would just have to carry on doing it. It was up to me to come to terms with the situation and make the best of it.

So I accepted what The Doc said, and lined up for United against Middlesbrough in the next match, which was a top-of-the-table battle in front of 60,000 fans at Old Trafford. And I was still in the side at the end of the month, when we played Ajax in the U.E.F.A. Cup. It was a game we won 2–0, and I was one of the scorers, though the real star of the night was Brian Greenhoff, who laid on the goal for me.

That was one of those games which goes to prove that the unexpected can happen in football. We had played Ajax in Holland and lost 1–0, and for the second leg at Old Trafford we were without Stuart Pearson, who was injured – so, like it or not, I was earmarked for a front-line job. But the game was still delicately poised at 1–1 on aggregate, after Lou Macari had scored, and Ajax remained in with a chance of snatching victory.

If nothing else, The Doc is a decision-maker, and he was bold enough to gamble by pulling off Gerry Daly, sending on Arthur Albiston to play in defence, and switching Brian Greenhoff forward to fill in for the midfield job vacated by Gerry. The gamble was that our reshuffled defence, with Arthur at left-back and Stewart Houston taking Brian's place at the heart of the defence, would be able to keep a grip on the Ajax attackers, while Brian Greenhoff supplied the driving force for us to push forward. And it worked.

From the moment Brian moved upfield, he couldn't put a foot wrong, and when he broke down the right with Steve Coppell, the move ended with a cross which left me needing only to apply the finishing touch. And so we scored an aggregate, 2–1 victory.

That was a happy experience for Brian, who is a good friend of mine – happier than one he had when United were touring 'down under'. And let me say here that while I'm the first to appreciate that if it hadn't been for professional football, I would never have travelled around the world (and all expenses paid, at that), if you think it's one long round of glamour, when you set off for a trip to Europe or the Far East, you can forget it.

I can assure you that not only is there plenty of hard work, even when you are playing so-called friendly matches, but that you can soon become travel-weary. When we made the journey to Australia, we did it in a roundabout way, first stopping off to play a game in Tehran, then flying across the ocean to take in Indonesia, Hong Kong and, finally, arriving tired out in Australia.

Which was where – in Sydney, to be precise – Brian Green-hoff suffered one of the most frightening experiences of his life . . . and, in a way, I suppose I was responsible for the scare he got.

I was rooming with Brian, and one evening in the hotel I really fancied something to eat, but by that time, the restaurant had closed down. So I suggested it wouldn't be a bad idea if we brought some fish and chips – you can get those in any country! – from a shop which was just down the road. Brian very kindly volunteered to go for them.

A little while later he returned, complete with fish and chips – but he was breathless, and one look at his chalk-white face told me that he hadn't run all the way back just for fun. 'What's the matter?' I asked him, adding: 'You look as white as a sheet.' And when he began to explain, no wonder.

It turned out that just as he was being served, he became very much aware of an Aussie behind him in the queue. The Digger had fairly obviously been plying himself with drinks before he visited the 'chippy', and he must have cottoned on to Brian's accent as my team-mate gave his order.

At any rate, first of all the Aussie made no secret of the fact that he wasn't particularly fond of Englishmen, and Brian began to become a bit worried as to how far the guy was prepared to take his dislike, on account of the way he was slating those 'so-and-so Pommies' . . . but what really put the wind up my room-mate was when this character suddenly pulled a gun on him.

Fortunately, by then Brian had the fish and chips wrapped up and in his hands, and he didn't waste any time on seeing whether there was to be a sequel. He hurriedly handed over the cash to the person behind the counter, and didn't linger one second longer. He just made himself scarce, and rushed back to the safety of the hotel.

I couldn't help but burst out laughing as Brian told me the story, while the look on his face indicated so clearly that HE had found it anything but a laughing matter, while he was in the chip shop. And he left me in no doubt that he reckoned I had got my priorities all wrong when I said to him: 'Thank goodness you didn't drop the fish and chips!'

While we were 'down under' our programme included a match against the Australian national side, and it contained several of the men who had been to the World Cup finals, but United had little trouble in chalking up a 4–0 victory, although I will say the Aussies put up some pretty determined resistance when it came to the physical aspects of the game. Indeed, for one or two of our opponents the motto seemed to be 'If it moves, then kick it!'

Our travels took us to Sydney, Perth and Melbourne – we spent three days in each of these fair Australian cities – and then we were on the move again, this time flying across to New Zealand. So it really was a matter of living out of a suitcase all the time, and as our Soccer safari occupied five weeks, there was plenty of dirty laundry piling up. At one stage, there developed a bit of an argument about the laundry, and who should be paying for it, but The Doc was adamant that the players would have to foot the bill themselves.

On the way back to Britain – and you can believe me when I say we were very happy to embark on the homeward leg, after our travels which had taken us over thousands of miles – we touched down in Los Angeles, and stayed overnight at the Beverley Hilton. That was a magnificent hotel, indeed, and some of the lads were a little bit sick that our stopover was so brief. But they perked up again when we touched down for a five-day rest in Bermuda.

That, without the shadow of a doubt, is the nicest place I have ever visited – and I've travelled around. In Europe I have seen the sights of France, Holland, Belgium, Germany, Italy, Spain, Portugal, Norway, Denmark, Sweden, Bulgaria and Yugoslavia; and I've seen a fair part of the Far East. But Bermuda really is something special, with its balmy atmosphere and its air of luxury.

For once, I was reluctant to leave, but while our team-mates were staying on for another couple of days, Paddy Roche and myself were boarding a plane after 72 hours in this sunshine paradise, because we had a date in Ireland, for we had promised to attend Gerry Daly's wedding in Dublin. And if that fair city is not quite as exotic as Bermuda, I must confess that we had a jolly good time as we wished Gerry and his bride a happy future and sampled the hospitality at the reception.

15   The Irish Angle

Five managers at Manchester United, four at international level . . . so no-one can say I haven't had to be adaptable! The man who first gave me my chance with Northern Ireland was Terry Neill, and when I first met him and heard him speak, I must admit I couldn't make up my mind whether he was an American or an Irishman, for his accent seemed to be laced with a definite twang. Not only is he a smooth talker, of course; his record shows that apart from having collected 59 international caps as a player, he has done well in the game as a manager.

It was at the beginning of January, in 1972, that I first became a candidate for an international cap, after a handful of games for Manchester United which were marked by goals. Terry Neill had plenty of things on his mind around that time, for as manager of Hull City, he was concerned with ensuring that they didn't slip down to the Third Division, while as the team boss of the Irish international side, he was planning his strategy for the European Nations Cup-tie against Spain which was due to take place at Boothferry Park the following month.

His club commitments meant that he hadn't had time to do much checking on players for the game against Spain, so only a month before that match he still hadn't seen what I could do in First Division football, though he had got a glimpse of me in the odd match which had been televised. He had also conferred with United's manager at the time, Frank O'Farrell, and coach Malcolm Musgrove.

At that time, I was still playing most of my football in the reserves at Old Trafford, and it seemed too much to hope for that after only a few senior outings I would find myself wearing the green jersey of the international side. But Terry

Neill said he planned to cross the Pennines and watch me, and with Martin O'Neill and Sammy Morgan also being mentioned as candidates, you never knew your luck. Like me, Martin was in the reserves (at Nottingham Forest), while Sammy was playing in the lower divisions with Port Vale.

Northern Ireland's team boss, who was still a player himself, suggested that the time had come for some experiments with new faces, so I could only wait and hope . . . though when the big news did come, it wasn't from Terry Neill, but from my mother, who phoned my digs from Belfast to say she had heard a whisper that I was in. 'I'm sure it's true – but don't breathe a word to anybody until it comes out officially,' she warned me.

That was easier said than done, but for 18 hours I managed to keep quiet about what I had been told. I even got through a full training session with my United team-mates without letting on, although I have to admit that I was bursting to tell someone. But finally came the official announcement of the squad, and I knew for certain that, at 17, I had become an international footballer.

Fifteen players had been named for the match against Spain, but only five of them were forwards, and they included George Best, Derek Dougan and Eric McMordie, while Martin O'Neill and Sammy Morgan were also in the squad. The odds seemed on me getting a place in the side which kicked off against the Spaniards, especially since Northern Ireland knew in advance that they had failed to qualify for the final stages of the Nations Cup tournament, so the game could be used to put newcomers through their paces.

After only eight full senior games, I had made the breakthrough . . . and Terry Neill still hadn't seen me in action, except on TV. At 17 years and 198 days old, I became the second-youngest British footballer to claim an international cap – Norman Kernoghan, of the old Belfast Celtic club, was 118 days younger than me when he made his debut in 1936.

I made sure I was on the 8.40 am train from Manchester's Victoria station, even though George Best missed it, and I arrived to find that I would be rooming with Martin O'Neill, so two new boys were given the chance to get to know each other, as well as their team-mates. And for Terry Neill it was a hectic day, for apart from the non-arrival of George Best, he learned that Allan Hunter and Bryan Hamilton, both from Ipswich, had missed a train connection so they would be late getting to Hull.

As for George, whose failure to meet me at the station in Manchester meant that I had to dash and get my own ticket (I caught the train by a matter of seconds), the Irish star asked one of his business partners to drive him across to Hull . . . then the car broke down. But eventually George did turn up.

The game itself left me feeling a little bit disappointed with my own performance, for I felt I should have scored in the first few minutes – but I volleyed the ball over the bar.

However, most people seemed to think that I had had a highly satisfactory debut, and I certainly learned on my international bow that playing against foreign opposition can be even tougher than against teams in the First Division. The Spaniards handed out some rough treatment, at times, especially with their tackling from behind, and several times I found myself on the floor, after being caught on the back of my legs and my heels, while George Best reacted angrily on one occasion when he was chopped down from the back.

The fellow who was marking me had the build of a wrestler, and he stuck closer to me than any opponent had ever done before, so that I found I never got room to turn with the ball. But at least I got some satisfaction from the fact that one free-kick awarded for a foul against me produced the equaliser, which was scored by Sammy Morgan. Spain's goal came from a breakaway – one of only three real scoring attempts they had in the 90 minutes, for they spent most of their time concentrating on massed defence.

I was still playing for Manchester United's youth team, an occasional first-teamer, and an international footballer who was dropped after one appearance, for when the home-international championships came along, Terry Neill abandoned his experimental line-up in favour of experience and a 4–4–2 formation for the first match, against Scotland at

Hampden Park. George Best had been dropped, and also on the outside looking in were myself, Martin O'Neill and Sammy Morgan. But my turn came again, and I went on to play for Northern Ireland as a regular, even though the managership of the team changed two or three times.

I owe Terry Neill something for giving me my international debut, and we have never had a cross word. But although Terry puts himself over well, I cannot say that I really enjoyed my spell in the international side when he was the team boss.

He's a great one for diagrams and tactics, and it seemed to me that every 15 minutes or so there were team meetings and sessions involving the blackboard. Then again, maybe I was biased because he didn't pick me when I thought I should have been in the side – I remember him dropping me and playing Willie Irvine, who was then coming towards the close of his career, and I wouldn't have been human if I hadn't held that against Terry.

When I was axed for the three home international matches, after my debut against Spain, he didn't explain why I had been left out, and though these games might have been important, from a prestige point of view, I felt that they were good ones for the younger players to sample, and good ones in which to continue the experiments. Now that I've played around three dozen matches for Northern Ireland, I still feel the same way, and you have my word for it that when I was substitute both for Manchester United and Northern Ireland, it was one of the most difficult spells of my career. I'd rather play for the reserves than sit on the bench as a substitute.

When Dave Clements was appointed as successor to Terry Neill, he did a good job, for my money, though I reckon someone managing a side on a part-time basis has more problems than he needs. I felt Dave worked as hard as he could at making a go of things, and I was a bit sorry when he was no longer the international manager . . . though I have to add that I had no regrets about Danny Blanchflower's spell in charge.

To me, he was really just a name – I'd read about his achievements as a player in the Tottenham side which did the double during the early part of the 1960's, and I knew he had worn the Irish jersey with distinction. But he was like those other greats of the past, Peter Doherty and Jimmy McIlroy – still little more than a name.

Now that I've seen Danny Blanchflower at close quarters, and worked under his management, I know him a lot better, and in my opinion he did put Northern Ireland football on the map, internationally speaking. And he was ably assisted by the No. 2 at Old Trafford, Tommy Cavanagh. I think they had a good squad of players and there was tremendous team spirit, and I learned quite a bit when Danny was in charge.

He talks well – show me an Irishman who doesn't – and obviously enjoyed his involvement in the game. He also wanted us to win matches, and when we pulled off a good result, the expression on his face told its own story. At the same time, he never forgot that it's important the players should enjoy their football, and he always took pains to remind us that no-one was putting us under pressure. Danny's motto, really, was that we should be relaxed, and that this should show in the way we played our football.

Cav is a man who, in a sense, provides the sergeant-major touch, for he's a stickler for discipline, while Danny brought the voice of quiet reason to the proceedings. As a matter of fact, we had two Danny Blanchflowers at international get-togethers, for striker Derek Spence does a take-off of the original Danny to perfection . . . and on occasion it's been known for us to listen to two team talks, one from Danny, and the other from Derek. Not surprisingly, though, Derek Spence always tried to make sure that Danny wasn't around when he was giving us the blarney!

If Derek Spence is a comedian deliberately, Terry Cochrane often introduces a note of humour into the proceedings when he's being serious, and this unconscious style of wit brings him a ribbing from his team-mates. We call Terry 'Steptoe', and sometimes it's just like a scene from the TV series when Terry and a team-mate get going.

There was one occasion when Derek Spence found his impression of Danny Blanchflower too close to home, and it happened when we were playing in Belfast and we were all told to report in a certain room at the hotel for the team talk. The lads got Derek up to do his piece before Danny arrived, and we had the blackboard set up, with Derek drawing diagrams while we sat lolling about in chairs. Suddenly, Danny Blanchflower walked in, and there was a gale of laughter from the players, while Derek nipped to his own seat, muttering: 'Now he's caught me . . . that'll be the last time I'll play for Northern Ireland.' Needless to say, it wasn't, because Danny has a sense of humour, too.

Danny always enlivened the proceedings because he had a fund of stories about personalities of Irish teams gone by, and when he began talking of games in which he played, and related incidents that happened, he had us in stitches. One story concerns the 1958 World Cup in Sweden, where Northern Ireland became favourites with everyone as they played their football with a sense of adventure.

It seems the goalkeeper of one side was leaping about from one end of the goal to the other as he tried to line up his defence for a free-kick which was being taken outside the box. All the outfield players were standing and looking behind them, asking the 'keeper if they were in the right position . . . while the guy taking the kick just moved the ball a little bit, then bent the kick round the defensive wall while the 'keeper was still issuing orders to his team-mates.

From my own observations, every player who pulls on the green jersey takes real pride in wearing it, and none more so than Allan Hunter, the Ipswich defender, who not only loves playing for his country, but gives 100 per cent effort right through the 90 minutes – not that I'm suggesting his team-mates don't! On his day, Allan is one of the top centre-halves in the League, and with Kevin Beattie he forms one of the best defensive partnerships in British football.

Mention of Kevin reminds me that during my early days with Manchester United this fellow never used to give me a kick when Ipswich were playing at Old Trafford – so, naturally, I've respected him ever since, and I reckon that but for the injuries which have hampered his career, he would have been an established regular in the England team. In my book, he's like Allan Hunter – one of the top defenders in the game.

When Kevin Beattie is missing from the Ipswich team, it puts a great deal of pressure on Allan Hunter; together, they make a formidable combination, and I wouldn't have minded seeing the pair of them wearing the Irish jersey. I wish Jimmy Greaves had been born in a later era, and in Northern Ireland, as well, because the only thing we've been lacking in recent years has been firepower – someone to tuck away the scoring chances we have created.

With Northern Ireland, I've played against countries such as Spain, Bulgaria, Holland, Belgium, Sweden, Denmark, Norway, Portugal and Yugoslavia, and I'll remember the game against the Yugoslavs because of a booking I received for a little gesture I made to the referee. He awarded us a free-kick, despite the chorus of whistling from the Yugoslav fans, and I was so pleased that he hadn't been swayed by the hostile crowd that I patted him on the head. My reward was the yellow card.

The Yugoslavs don't really regard themselves as being behind the Iron Curtain, and there is certainly a difference between that country and one or two others – Bulgaria, for example, which I have now visited on two occasions. The first time I went with Northern Ireland, we spent three days there, and I found it a grey and rather depressing – or maybe I should say depressed – country. When I went there for the second time, it struck me that nothing much seemed to have improved, five years on.

I've played at international level against more than a few world-class stars, and I was impressed very much by Allan Simonsen when he was in action for Denmark against us. I haven't been at all surprised by his success with the various Continental clubs for which he has played, because although he is by no means a giant in stature, he showed he has a very sharp eye for an opening, and he lacks nothing in courage, as well as ability.

Another Scandinavian star also impressed me when he was playing against Northern Ireland. That was Freeling Lund, who became a target for Real Madrid, Ajax and Feyenoord, among others. He was outstanding in a game against us, for after we had taken a 1–0 lead, Lund simply took the game by the scruff of the neck and beat us on his own, as he scored a couple of fine goals.

It was while I was on tour with Manchester United that I first came across star Dutch names such as Rep, Krol, Neeskens and Suurbier, and the venue for a game against Ajax of Amsterdam was, of all places, Indonesia. That day, United were without five of their first-team regulars, who were on duty with Scotland, and we produced a tremendous display, considering that the average age of our side was something like 18. The Dutch aces were quite happy to wind up winning by the odd goal in five.

At international level, Johan Cruyff showed us more than a few samples of his skill, when we played Holland during the World Cup qualifying matches before Argentina, but I must admit that while Neeskens turned on the style when we met Ajax at club level in Indonesia, I was disappointed with the way he performed against Northern Ireland during a World Cup-tie in Amsterdam.

That day, Neeskens' mission in life seemed to be to make sure that George Best received as much stick as possible during the whole of the 90 minutes, and I felt that a player of the Dutch star's reputation and skill really shouldn't have needed to go in like that, even though he might have been instructed to make sure he kept on breathing down George's neck. Since his move to Barcelona, it appears to me that Neeskens' role has been altered – he has seemed to be much more of a marker than the creative midfield player he once was with Ajax, and I felt this was very much in evidence, also, when Barcelona won the final of the European Cup-winners Cup against Fortuna Dusseldorf in the spring of 1979.

I've mentioned the players of Juventus elsewhere – and undoubtedly the roughest, toughest guy with whom I've ever tried conclusions was Tardelli, the Italian international, who spent a great deal of his time giving me some very special attention. For the most part, he was content to keep on tugging my jersey, and once he elbowed me in the eye when the ball was nowhere near either of us. Certainly I won't forget coming up against Signor Tardelli and his team-mates in a hurry.

I remember another game for Northern Ireland, too, when we played England in Belfast, and after they had beaten us 2–1 at Windsor Park, their team manager at the time, Don Revie, paid us the compliment of saying we had been unlucky, adding: 'We were a bit frightened of you.' To which Danny Blanchflower replied: 'How can you be frightened of us? – We haven't beaten you in Belfast in 50 years!'

If there have been things to regret about playing for Northern Ireland, one is the fact that the troubles back home have meant that other countries have not been over-keen to visit Belfast for international games, and that, indeed, was why I made my debut for my country at Boothferry Park. I wished it could have been at Windsor Park, but you can't have everything.

Another reason for regret is that truly great footballers such as George Best and Pat Jennings have never been to the finals of the World Cup – talent such as theirs deserved to grace the great moments of the tournament, as millions of people around the world get a ringside seat via television.

George didn't always do himself justice in an Irish shirt, and maybe part of the reason was that he lacked the incentive, in that he could be pretty certain Northern Ireland would never get past the qualifying rounds and the most he could expect was to star in home internationals and the odd game against a foreign side. I'm just putting forward a theory, of course, and I'm not forgetting that he turned in some memorable displays, notably when we played Holland in Amsterdam and came away with a 2–2 draw.

Pat Jennings has defied the years as he has starred for club and country, and I feel sure that if he had played in the final rounds of a World Cup competition he would have been a strong contender for the best goalkeeper award.

I suppose it's one of the disappointments of my footballing career, too, that I haven't been able to go to Munich or Argentina, but maybe I'll wind up as a member of a Northern Ireland team which does make it all the way. But whether I do or not, I would still prefer to play for Northern Ireland rather than see a Great Britain side, as some people have urged over the years.

I wouldn't dispute that if Great Britain played in the World Cup, the team would probably qualify for the finals every four years, but I don't think it would be quite the same – and selecting a team manager and a team from the four home countries would be a task for Solomon himself. Just imagine the arguments as to whether the goalkeeping position should go to Pat Jennings or Ray Clemence, for instance; and try picking the outfield players from a list of about 40 candidates!

Scottish fans wouldn't want a Sassenach in the side, for starters!

They say it's an ill wind which blows nobody any good, and my international career took a new turning with the appointment of Billy Bingham as Northern Ireland's team manager, for he named me as team captain for the home internationals in the spring of 1980, in time for Northern Ireland to finish on top of the home championship table for the first time in many years. And he paid me a handsome tribute when he said I was 'the sort of man I would pick to have beside me in the trenches . . . invariably cool, reliable and respected.'

The sting was in the tail, as he added : 'I do feel he should score more often for us – two goals so far in 40 internationals are not enough.' A sentiment with which I agreed, as we prepared for the first game, against Scotland in Belfast. I must admit that being named captain was, for me, the high point of my international career, and I like to think that I justified Billy's faith in me.

16   Red for Danger

I'll admit it . . . I was somewhat apprehensive as to what season 1979–80 would bring for Manchester United, even though we had rounded off the previous term by playing in the F.A. Cup final against Arsenal. Quite simply, United had not been at all convincing in the League even as were going to Wembley, and I knew that at that start of a new campaign, many people would be looking at us with critical eyes.

We had made some massive investments in the transfer market: Gordon McQueen, Joe Jordan, Mickey Thomas had cost a total of £1,200,000, and the arrival of Ray Wilkins from Chelsea took the outlay to the £2M mark. For that sort of money, folk were expecting something – and it had better be good!

Well, we had our setbacks between August, 1979, and May, 1980; but by the time the season was drawing to a close my worries had evaporated, for United were chasing Liverpool all the way for the First Division championship . . . and no matter what anyone might claim, they couldn't put it all down to good luck on our part. No question about it : we had earned whatever we had achieved.

I imagine that people might just say we had nothing left but the League, after our dismissal by Tottenham Hotspur from the F.A. Cup, and perhaps they have a point, because Liverpool became involved in a battle to reach the final of the League Cup, the final of the F.A. Cup, and to clinch the League title. So right up to the late stages of the season they had plenty on their plate.

Yet, having conceded this, I maintain that United showed, in the last two months of their campaign, that they could stick it out and stay the pace. And don't forget that right the way through the season, we had been one of the few clubs genuinely disputing the title issue with Liverpool. After four matches we were third, after five we were second, and after half a dozen we had hit the top.

From then on until mid-November, when Liverpool became the leaders for the first time, we were never out of the top three; and we leap-frogged over Liverpool to regain the leadership until they climbed back on December 8 . . . and stayed there week after week, until the last matches on the fixture list began to loom. Yet United remained right on their heels, in second position, and we refused to be overtaken by the likes of Ipswich and Arsenal.

Eventually, it became clear that it was indeed a two-horse race for the title, although towards the end of March, everyone outside Old Trafford was dismissing our part in the affair, for Liverpool had gone half a dozen points clear, and the bookies were refusing to take any more bets, since they clearly regarded the Anfield Reds as racing certainties.

But by the last Saturday of the season, the position was still delicately balanced, and the points gap had been whittled away.

I've got to hand it to manager Dave Sexton, for when everyone was ruling us out, he kept on saying – and publicly – that Manchester United hadn't given up the chase. He was realistic, for he admitted that we had to win every single one of our remaining matches, and even then we were looking for Liverpool to slip. But he drove us on by his refusal to concede that the championship was already in Liverpool's keeping.

Looking back, I find that there were days to remember and days to forget. In the November, we hammered Norwich City 5–0 and scored our biggest victory of the season to regain the leadership of the First Division. Joe Jordan scored two goals that day, and in the later stages of the campaign he was to win praise not only for his goals, but for his all-round play.

Joe arrived at Old Trafford with a big-money tag round his neck, and a reputation as a fellow whose aerial power was something special, but who wasn't in the top bracket as a marksman, considering all the games he had played for

Leeds. By the end of the season, he was playing better than at any time in his career, had improved his game on the ground tremendously, and was winning acclaim both for the goals he was scoring and for his all-round footballing skills.

There were games when we had to rely upon fighting spirit to produce something for us. When we played Crystal Palace at Old Trafford, Dave Swindlehurst rocked us by putting Palace in front, and there were only 10 minutes left for us to preserve an unbeaten home record when Joe struck an equaliser. It marked his return to the side after a spell of injury which had meant him missing 10 matches.

Tottenham are one team I'll remember, for when we went to White Hart Lane for the League game, we came away smiling, after Lou Macari and Steve Coppell had scored, to clinch a 2–1 victory. Then we had to go back for an F.A. Cup-tie, and when Ossie Ardiles scored it seemed we were on the way out. However, I scored from the penalty spot, and once more we left White Hart Lane laughing, as we looked forward to applying the killer blow in the replay.

We were confident, all right, because apart from anything else, we had a pretty good record against Spurs, and we felt that we had done the hard bit. That replay taught us once more the lesson that in this game, nothing must be taken for granted. Spurs came to Old Trafford with grit in their teeth; they survived the hammer blow of having goalkeeper Milija Aleksic carried off; and just as we were getting ready to settle for a draw, Ardiles whacked in a late winner.

On the night, we had had the chances to win, but we couldn't take anything from Spurs, sick at heart though we were. Our consolation came towards the end of the season when Spurs returned to Old Trafford for the second League encounter, and Andy Ritchie – playing only his second full League game of the season – rapped in a hat-trick as we hammered Spurs 4–1.

The 99th derby game between United and Manchester City was at Maine Road, and that was a sickener for us, as City – struggling though they were in the League – defied the tipsters by beating us 2–0, with goals from Tony Henry and Mike Robinson. Gary Bailey saved us from further

F

goals, Steve Coppell hit the woodwork, and on a mudbath of a pitch we sank to defeat.

I'll confess that I feel we went into that derby game with a totally wrong attitude. City were having such a bad time and we were way up the table . . . in my book, we went into the match feeling too complacent by half. So we learned another lesson. And when the return game was played at Old Trafford, we didn't take it lightly at all.

Then, we were only too thankful for a Mickey Thomas drive which was deflected past 'keeper Joe Corrigan by Tony Henry. It turned out to be the game's only goal, and prised two precious points from our great rivals.

As the season wore on, we learned that fighting spirit can salvage something from a match which is beginning to look beyond you. For instance, when Leeds came to Old Trafford, their young scoring sensation, Terry Connor, stunned the United faithful – and there were 57,478 people on the ground – by sticking a goal past us after only 22 minutes. Leeds had their tails up, and it took us the best part of an hour to snatch a point-saver, after Ashley Grimes had failed to do the trick from the penalty spot.

That wasn't the first or the last time we had a crowd of 57,000 at Old Trafford during the season, although the visit of Leeds produced the top First Division gate of the season – and it was notable also for the fact that it was estimated 2,000 fans had to be locked out.

We had spells when key players such as Gordon McQueen and Joe Jordan were out through injury, and I must say that lads like Kevin Moran and Ashley Grimes contributed a great deal to our overall performance when you weigh up the season. Ashley himself had injury problems later on, but he did a great job when standing-in for Mickey Thomas.

As for Mickey, he went from strength to strength. He would be the first to admit that when he arrived at Old Trafford, he felt a bit overawed by the names he saw around him. So he lacked a bit of confidence, and reckoned that his real strength was simply as a player who could keep on grafting and running. But he settled down to show that he wasn't simply a workhorse; he made goals and scored them, and still managed to maintain his ability to chase and cover in the midfield area of the park.

Kevin Moran arrived at United as a player who had gained fame in Ireland at another sport – Gaelic football. He was an All-Ireland man, and – not surprisingly – a few eyebrows were raised when he decided to make the switch and take his chance as a professional soccer player. Gordon McQueen's absence because of injury saw Kevin flung in at the deep end, and he soon proved that he had what it took – he quickly made it apparent that he was a rock-hard centre-back. Before the season had ended, he had repeated his international success in Gaelic football by winning honours with the Republic of Ireland Soccer team.

If United preserved their unbeaten home record by pinching a point from Crystal Palace, we certainly proved we could do better, by giving both Nottingham Forest and Arsenal a 3–0 beating. Gordon McQueen was a marksman against Forest at Old Trafford, and Joe Jordan struck twice, to take his tally to five goals in half a dozen matches. Then, against Arsenal, Joe made it six goals in eight matches, Gordon scored his seventh of the season – and I tucked away a chance from the penalty spot.

That fighting spirit? – It brought us a point at Middlesbrough and at Stoke. The game at Ayresome came after our F.A. Cup exit, but we showed we weren't suffering from any hangover, and Mickey Thomas was the man whose goal produced a 1–1 result, while Steve Coppell equalised seven minutes from time at Stoke.

I mentioned setbacks, and we had one at Old Trafford against Wolves, who were destined to beat Nottingham Forest in the final of the League Cup shortly afterwards. Some people seemed to think that with a Wembley date on their minds, Wolves would be easy meat for United – but our unbeaten home record went to the wall as Mel Eves scored in the first half. Although I had a shot scrambled clear, we were really off colour that afternoon, and the news that Liverpool had won 5–3 at Norwich didn't make for any improvement in our condition.

Against that, we went to the Baseball Ground and made

things go our way against Derby County. That game marked the debut for United of our Yugoslav signing, Nikola Jovanovic, and while he found his baptism of English football a bit hard going, it worked out right for us all in the end. Derby went ahead, but Mickey Thomas levelled the score, then I settled the issue with a penalty goal a couple of minutes from time. Just to add the icing to the cake, Barry Powell put through his own goal to give us a final, 3–1 scoreline.

However, not every away trip ended on such a happy note for United, and Saturday, March 1, was the worst day of the season for us, because we played Ipswich at Portman Road and finished up feeling shell-shocked. It was a disaster, in terms of goals. Two minutes gone, and Alan Brazil opened the scoring; two more goals from Paul Mariner, and it was Ipswich (already unbeaten in 15 matches) winning 3–0. Not only that, but Gary Bailey had saved one penalty from Frans Thijssen and a twice-taken spot-kick from Kevin Beattie.

Well, we did harbour some thoughts about going out and making a game of it in the second half, but the agony was to be repeated as Ipswich set about us again. Brazil scored to make it a brace of goals for himself, Thijssen struck goal No. 5, and Mariner came up with a sixth which gave him a hat-trick. To make things even worse, we learned that Liverpool had gone to Goodison Park and inflicted a 2–1 defeat on Everton.

If we had needed to make a comeback after our F.A. Cup defeat by Spurs, we certainly had to recover from that six-goal mauling at Ipswich. A mid-week clash with Everton at Old Trafford brought us a point, and a trip to Brighton on the Saturday produced another scoreless draw. They weren't exactly inspired performances by United, but they got us back on the rails.

That 100th derby game against Manchester City produced a 1–0 win for us at Old Trafford, and – with Liverpool half a dozen points clear and nine matches to go – manager Dave Sexton was spelling it out for us. We had to hit a winning streak and maintain it. When we played at Selhurst Park the following Saturday, we knew it would be a tough one, but goals from Joe Jordan and Mickey Thomas earned us a win, while a few miles away Liverpool were losing 2–0 to Spurs at White Hart Lane. That cut the points gap to four.

The following Tuesday night, Liverpool managed to beat Stoke 1–0 at Anfield, and although they didn't give one of their most fluent displays, the result widened the gap at the top to half a dozen points again . . . with Manchester United getting their chance to do something about it 24 hours later, when we played Nottingham Forest at the City Ground.

It's a game I prefer to forget, because I lost my head and received marching orders from referee Clive Thomas. Apart from that, United finished up on the wrong end of a 2–0 scoreline. So it seemed that there was nothing we could do to bridge that points gap between ourselves and Liverpool.

We had given Forest a bit of a chasing on our own ground back in the December, but when you take on Brian Clough's team at the City Ground you are realistic enough to think that getting a point is a good result, and winning is something you dream about. For United, a point would have been satisfactory; and as the game entered the final stretch, we were looking capable of prising one out of Forest.

However, referee Thomas decided that Forest should be awarded a penalty, and my protests not only went unheeded . . . they brought me marching orders. I still feel that the decision wasn't correct, but at the time I wasn't recognising the stark, simple fact of football life – that once the referee has made his decision, you cannot do anything to reverse it.

We had been under pressure for much of the game, and we were coming close to holding out for a draw and a point which could prove priceless, in the final analysis. When the penalty was awarded, reason flew out of the window, so far as I was concerned, and I'll admit now that this was because I felt the penalty would bring about our defeat. John Robertson's record as a spot-kick taker was impressive, and I didn't believe he would pass up this gilt-edged chance. He didn't . . . and when Gary Birtles scored for Forest in the last couple of minutes, my cup of personal woe was overflowing.

I knew that, automatically, I would miss the next match because of having been sent off. And it was a sad and sorry Sammy McIlroy who travelled back to Manchester. No doubt about it : I was in a chastened mood.

My suspension took immediate effect . . . and the game I had to miss was the one at Old Trafford which could prove to be the 'crunch' fixture, for our opponents were Liverpool. If they got anything out of that one, with a six-point lead already in their grasp, Manchester United could surely kiss the championship good-bye.

Dave Sexton took a gamble – and it paid off handsomely. Jimmy Greenhoff, the man whose F.A. Cup semi-final goal in a Goodison replay had put paid to Liverpool and taken United to Wembley the previous spring, was named in the side to face the men from Anfield. Jimmy was 33, and it would be his first full match since the F.A. Cup final.

More than that, it marked the return of a player who had been medically advised to hang up his playing boots, after a long and painful battle to overcome a pelvic injury. But now fate had pitched him into another confrontation with the team he had 'jinxed' the previous season.

When Kenny Dalglish struck for Liverpool with fewer than 15 minutes gone, the League championship battle certainly looked to be swaying their way. Gordon McQueen went in for the tackle, and Dalglish skipped clear, then drew 'keeper Gary Bailey before sliding home a typical effort. However, five minutes later United had drawn level, thanks to Mickey Thomas.

Maybe there was an element of good fortune about it, from our point of view, for Steve Coppell sped down the right and beat full-back Alan Kennedy, who pulled up sharply as he was about to get in the tackle. Kennedy seemed to have pulled a muscle, but Steve didn't stop to inquire. He produced a superb centre which Mickey Thomas, at the second attempt, forced past 'keeper Ray Clemence.

Kennedy went off, young Sammy Lee was brought into the action for Liverpool, but from the moment we had levelled the score, we began to gain the upper hand. It was still 1–1 at half-time, but with just over an hour gone, Jimmy Greenhoff once more had his moment of glory. Steve Coppell took a corner, Joe Jordan headed the ball goalwards

. . . and Jimmy got his head to the ball to put it past Clemence.

So it was six games to go, and Liverpool were on 52 points, United on 48. The gap had been reduced from six to four points, and 48 hours later United could whittle it down to two, providing they won at Burnden Park against Bolton, who were virtually already doomed to relegation. At half-time it was 1–1, but the final scoreline showed that goals from Gordon McQueen, Mickey Thomas and Steve Coppell had done the trick for United.

Now we had to wait and see what Liverpool could do against Derby County – another club in peril of taking the drop – at Anfield the following night. Liverpool obliged their anxious supporters by sticking three goals past Derby, and so it became a four point gap once more.

The following Saturday, Liverpool were trying their luck against Arsenal at Hillsborough, in the semi-finals of the F.A. Cup, while United were at home to Spurs. Andy Ritchie's hat-trick and a goal from Ray Wilkins made it a 4–1 win for us, and suddenly, the gap had been narrowed to a couple of points, though Liverpool had five games to play, against our four. For the first time, people outside Manchester seemed to take the threat from United seriously, especially as Liverpool and Arsenal had to replay after a scoreless draw in the Cup. And, as it turned out, that semi-final was to stretch into a marathon . . .

The following Wednesday, Liverpool and Arsenal drew their replay, 1–1, at Villa Park. The following Saturday, United won 2–0 against Norwich at Carrow Road, thanks to a brace of goals from Joe Jordan, while Liverpool were dropping a point in a 1–1 draw against Arsenal – this time in the League – at Anfield. Just one point between us now, though the Anfield Reds still had four games left to our three, and a superior goal difference. We were relying on them to come unstuck while we had to carry on winning.

The following Wednesday, we played our 40th game of the season in the League, and against Aston Villa at Old Trafford we managed to wind up with the better of things, in a match that saw three goals scored. Twice Joe Jordan struck, to give us the edge . . . but meantime, Liverpool were putting two goals past Stoke at the Victoria Ground.

So the last Saturday of April arrived, and Liverpool were getting bogged down in their efforts to reach Wembley, as well as claim the title for the second successive season and the 12th time in their history. They had had injury problems, too, with Jimmy Case, Terry McDermott and Alan Kennedy out of action. We could only hope that we won, and won again, while all Liverpool's efforts in Cup and League drained them to the point where they failed to get results.

You had to admire their dogged persistence, especially in view of their injuries, and I would have loved to see them beating Arsenal and winning the Cup, so long as we inched our way to the title. On that last Saturday in April, Liverpool had their work cut out to pull off a 0–0 draw against Crystal Palace at Selhurst Park, while United were winning 2–1 at home against Coventry. And that game produced another controversy.

Referee George Courtney awarded us a penalty after play had been going for only five minutes, and I duly despatched the spot-kick past Jim Blyth. Coventry protested that Steve Coppell's fall hadn't merited a penalty, and all I can say is that from where I was – a fair distance away – it seemed that Steve had the beating of his opponent and had got the ball past him when he was downed. Admittedly, Steve was going pretty fast, but I saw no reason to argue about the award of a spot-kick.

When Coventry equalised, things began to look serious for United, then we were awarded a free-kick. At the time, I was concerned with only one thing – making that award pay off in the shape of a goal. I had practised taking free-kicks from similar situations, and I was determined to do my damnedest to beat Jim Blyth. Frankly, I didn't notice that referee Courtney had raised an arm, and in my opinion it was a direct free-kick. So I slammed the ball goalwards, and it went round the wall of defenders and into the net, to give us a 2–1 victory and put United level on points with Liverpool.

I watched the television replay of the game that night, and Jimmy Hill raised two points: the referee had had his arm up to signal what looked like an indirect free-kick, and the film also showed what appeared to be an offence by Jimmy Greenhoff, as the kick was taken, for Coventry's Tommy Hutchison whirled round as Jimmy left the end of the defensive wall and darted behind it. The argument was that Jimmy had pulled Tommy Hutchison with him.

Obviously, I saw nothing to suggest this when I was taking the kick, and – having seen the T.V. replay – my argument is that such things are part and parcel of the game.

The suggestion was that at least one dubious incident could become significant, if the goal I had scored ensured the title going to Manchester United. Yet I can only repeat what I said earlier about the game against Nottingham Forest – the referee's decision is final, like it or not. Against Forest, I felt that we had paid the penalty; against Coventry, the verdict went United's way.

The fact remained that Liverpool and United were both on 58 points, with Liverpool still in the thick of the F.A. Cup semi-final, and having two League matches to play, while United's last fling would come with their trip to Elland Road to meet Leeds.

Liverpool's second replay against Arsenal was a dramatic affair, for Alan Sunderland gave the Gunners the lead after only 15 seconds, and Liverpool – down to 10 men after having lost David Johnson – equalised through Kenny Dalglish, with just 30 seconds to go. Extra time didn't resolve the stalemate, so a third replay was scheduled for the Thursday night at Coventry's Highfield Road ground.

The talk was that if there had to be yet another replay, it would go on at Bramall Lane the following Monday afternoon – just five days from the date of the final – and that meant Liverpool's League match against Middlesbrough at Ayresome Park would have to take place after the final, assuming they got to Wembley.

Meanwhile, while we were playing at Elland Road, they were coming up against Aston Villa at Anfield. If they won that match – though they must surely be wearied by their Cup exertions 48 hours earlier – nothing United could do at Leeds would make any difference. Liverpool would wind

up as champions, by beating Villa. So we waited on tenter-
hooks, first to see what happened in that third semi-final
replay . . .

This time, Arsenal got their noses in front and stayed
there. Brian Talbot scored early in the first half, Liverpool
powered back and tried to grind the Gunners into the ground
at Highfield Road – but the defence didn't wilt, and there was
no last-gasp reprieve goal by Kenny Dalglish to take the tie
into extra time again. Both teams were mentally and phy-
sically drained as they left the field, but Arsenal had the
knowledge that they would be going to Wembley for a record
third time in succession.

And Liverpool? – Two torrid Cup-ties in four days, and
a tussle with Villa for the championship prize 48 hours later;
that was their lot. Like everyone else in football, the players
at Old Trafford wondered if, at the eleventh hour, the League
prize would also be snatched from Liverpool's grasp. For if
we won at Leeds, and Liverpool failed to prise two points
from Villa at Anfield, there must surely be a doubt about their
ability to go to Ayresome Park the following Tuesday and pull
the chestnuts from the fire against Middlesbrough.

On grounds little more than 80 miles apart, the fans – more
than 91,000 of them – massed for the matches which could
decide matters. The gate at Anfield topped 51,000, and there
were almost 40,000 people at Elland Road. And inside the
first quarter of an hour, the signals were pointing towards
success for Liverpool, and gallant failure for Manchester
United, as David Johnson gave the Anfield Reds an early
lead and Derek Parlane struck a goal for Leeds.

Our hopes were raised briefly at half-time, even though
we were still trailing, for the scoreline at Anfield by then
read Liverpool 1, Aston Villa 1. But early in the second half,
Avi Cohen – whose own goal had put Villa level – scored
again, this time to give his team the lead.

A six-minute spell late in both matches settled things. At
Anfield, David Johnson scored his second and Liverpool's
third goal, after 72 minutes; at Elland Road, Kevin Hird
scored from the penalty spot after 76 minutes to make it
Leeds United 2, Manchester United 0; and back at Anfield,

after 78 minutes, a Ray Kennedy effort was deflected by a Villa player to make it Liverpool 4, Aston Villa 1. And so the First Division title was won and lost.

Manchester United's winning streak had come to an end, and Liverpool had mustered the strength for a final, winning fling. But although Leeds had raised their game and we hadn't been able to match them, at least we had finished as runners-up, and I felt that we had earned our place in Europe the following season.

We had also answered those critics who felt that Manchester United might be good enough to win six matches and claim a cup, but couldn't produce the necessary staying power over 42 League games. Apart from our promotion season, when we totalled 61 points as champions of the Second Division, our tally of 58 points was the highest United had achieved since before the dawn of the 1970's – and in another year it could have been good enough to claim the championship prize.

It equalled Manchester City's title-winning total of season 1967–68 and Derby County's tally in season 1971–72, and beat Derby's 1974–75 championship total by five points, and Liverpool's 1976–77 haul of 57 points. So we had some cause for pride, especially after the way we had whittled down that six-point lead which Liverpool had once held, and been the only other real contenders for the prize.

So the 1980's began on an auspicious note for Manchester United, as well as for Liverpool. Once again, they looked like being the team all the others had to beat . . . but United had served notice of their own intentions, and at Old Trafford we all felt that we could maintain the progress that had been made. Three trips to Wembley during the late stages of the 1970's, runners-up spot in the first term of a new decade. Yes, Manchester United are poised to be in the thick of the fight for honours and give their vast army of fans world-wide something to cheer. And I hope to be a part of that United bid for glory for a few more years to come!